W9-ACA-305

עָמוֹס הַיִּשְׂרְאֵלִי
Amos of Israel

עָמוֹס הַיִּשְׂרְאֵלִי
Amos of Israel
A New Interpretation

by Stanley N. Rosenbaum

PEETERS

MERCER

ISBN 0-86554-355-0

The paper used in the publication meets the minimum requirements
of American National Standard for Information Sciences—
Permanence of Paper for Printed Library Materials, ANSI Z39.48-1984.
∞

Library of Congress Cataloging-in-Publication Data
Rosenbaum, Stanley Ned, 1939–
Amos of Israel = ['Amos Yiśre'eli] : a new interpretation
by Stanley N. Rosebaum.
xii + 129pp. 6 × 9″ (15 × 23cm).
Includes bibliographical references.
ISBN 0-86554-355-0 (Mercer : alk. paper)
1. Amos (biblical prophet).
2. Bible, O.T. Amos—Criticism, interpretation, etc.
I. Title.   II. Title: 'Amos Yiśre'eli.
BS580.A6R67   1989   89-39065
224′.806—dc20   CIP

Contents

Maps

Dedication

*To our children
Sarah, William, Ephraim
conscious heirs to many traditions.*

Acknowledgments

Constructing a piece of biblical scholarship is a lot like building a pyramid: both take a long time and the finished product, attributed to one person, conceals the labor of many contributors. I wish, therefore, to acknowledge the efforts of those who gave so much of the straw with which my bricks were strengthened. While final responsibility for this edifice is mine, it is much better for their help and I remain deeply in their debt.

To my teachers, most especially J. Coert Rylaarsdam of the University of Chicago, and Nahum Glatzer, Nahum Sarna, and Cyrus Gordon of Brandeis—my thanks for introducing me to the tools of scholarship and for sharing their enthusiasm for using them. Each, I hope, will realize the extent of his influence in these pages, whether expressly acknowledged or not. I wish also to thank Professors Chaim Rabin and Menahem Haran of Hebrew University, Jerusalem, for early encouragement; Gosta Ahlstrom of Chicago; James Davila and Deborah Kennedy of Harvard; and Eric Meyers of Duke.

Dickinson colleagues who provided specific help from their fields of expertise include K. Robert Nilsson, political science; Robert Sider, classics; and Craig Houston, economics—and viticulture! Fellow laborers in the vineyard, the professors of religion who have been my friends for eighteen years, have shown enormous patience with my endless expositions through most of that time.

Dickinson provided me with a sabbatical supplement grant enabling me to spend a year as Fellow of the Institute for the Advanced Study of Religion at the University of Chicago Divinity School. I am grateful to George Allan and Franklin Gamwell, deans, respectively, of these two institutions. While I was at Chicago, Davidson Loehr took the jacket photograph of me, standing in front of the William Rainey Harper plaque.

An early verson of chapter 7 was presented at the JAOS-NACAL Conference in Seattle in March 1984. I thank colleagues there, especially Dennis Pardee of the Oriental Institute, for valuable suggestions leading to its improvement.

My editor at Mercer University Press has given the manuscript the benefit of much care and attention. His and his readers' suggestions—especially those of John I Durham—have greatly improved the text. Signal contributions have also been made by William D. Rosenbaum, who drew the two maps that appear on pages xii and 8. Barbara McDonald and Rosalie Lehman, secretaries in classics and religion, each gave considerable help with the manuscript, as did our student assistants, Kasey Kesselring, Brian Smith, and Helen Kwon.

Finally, I take great pleasure in acknowledging the debts owing to my mother z"l (*zichronah l'brachah*; may her memory be for a blessing) who always knew I would do it; and to my wife, Mary Helene Rosenbaum, who more than anyone else provided the spiritual environment—and much practical help with all phases of the project—to ensure I could.

—Ned Rosenbaum
Carlisle, Pennsylvania
30 June 1988

Principal Abbreviations

AASOR *Annual of the American Schools of Oriental Research*
AB Anchor Bible
AJSL *American Journal of Semitic Languages and Literatures*
ANET *Ancient Near Eastern Texts*, 3rd edition
AOS American Oriental Series
AV Authorized Version
BASOR *Bulletin of the American Schools of Oriental Research*
BHK *Biblia hebraica,* ed. Kittel et al., 3rd edition (1937ff.)
BHS *Biblia hebraica stuttgartensia* (1967–1977)
BM *Beth Miqra*
BT *The Bible Translator*
BTB *Biblical Theology Bulletin*
BZAW Beihefte zur *Zeitschrfit für die alttestamentliche Wissenschaft*
CBQ *Catholic Biblical Quarterly*
CIS *Corpus Inscriptionum Semiticarum*
DOTT *Documents from Old Testament Times*
EncJud *Encyclopedia Judaica*
EM *Encyclopedia Miqrait*
EvT *Evangelische Theologie*
ExpTim *Expository Times*
FRLANT *Forschungen zur Religion und Literatur des Alten und Neuen Testaments*
GKC Gesenius-Kautsch-Cowley, *Hebrew Grammar,* 2nd English ed. (1910ff.)
HAR *Hebrew Annual Review*
HS *Hebrew Studies*
HTR *Harvard Theological Review*
ICC *International Critical Commentary*
IEJ *Israel Exploration Journal*

JAAR   *Journal of the American Academy of Religion*
JAOS   *Journal of the American Oriental Society*
JB   *Jerusalem Bible* (1966)
JBL   *Journal of Biblical Literature*
JEA   *Journal of Egyptian Archaeology*
JNES   *Journal of Near Eastern Studies*
JPOS   *Journal of the Palestine Oriental Society*
JPSV   Jewish Publication Society Version (1917)
JQR   *Jewish Quarterly Review*
JSOT   *Journal for the Study of the Old Testament*
JSS   *Journal of Semitic Studies*
JT   Jerusalem Talmud
JTS   *Journal of Theological Studies*
KAI   *Kanaanaische und aramaische Inschriften*
MO   *Le Monde Oriental*
NBab   New Babylonian (language)
NEB   New English Bible
NJB   *New Jerusalem Bible* (1985)
NJPST   *New Jewish Publication Society TaNaK* (1985)
OTL   Old Testament Library
Or   *Orientalia* (Rome)
OTS   Oudtestamentische Studien
RA   *Revue d'assyriologie et d'archaeologie orientale*
RB   *Revue biblique*
RSV   Revised Standard Version
SH   *Scripta Hierosolymitana* (Jerusalem)
T   *Textus* (Jerusalem)
TB   Babylonian Talmud
TDNT   *Theological Dictionary of the New Testament*
TDOT   *Theological Dictionary of the Old Testament*
TR   Textus Receptus
TT   *Theologisch Tijdschrift*
VT   *Vetus Testamentum*
VTSup   *Vetus Testamentum* supplements
WHJP   *World History of the Jewish People*
ZAW   *Zeitschrift für die alttestamentliche Wissenschaft*
ZDPV   *Zeitschrift des deutschen Palastina-Vereins*
ZTK   *Zeitschrift für Theologie und Kirche*

Map 1   **Western Asia, circa 850–750 B.C.E.**

1

Introduction

1.

Amos commentary is a cacophony. Every aspect of the book and its author—or authors?—produces dissonance. For example, most scholars think Amos's career unfolded during a period of Northern Kingdom prosperity. Simon Cohen, however, holds that Jeroboam II's forces were fighting a desperate defensive battle against Aram.[1]

Again, some people look at Amos as a shrewd political commentator, a knowledgeable person with international vision and Olympian impartiality. Artur Weiser, however, followed by Menahem Haran, detects more than a whiff of nationalism in his words, while William A. Irwin reduces

[1]Simon Cohen, "The Political Background of the Words of Amos," HUCA 36 (1965): 153-60; also Menahem Haran, "The Rise and Decline of the Empire of Jeroboam ben Joash," VT 17 (1967): 266-80. The opposing view is represented by John Hayes and J. Maxwell Miller, eds. *Israelite and Judean History* (Philadelphia: Westminster; London: SCM, 1977) 414; Hans Walter Wolff, *Joel and Amos,* Hermeneia (Philadelphia: Fortress, 1977) 89; Haim Tadmor, "The Period of the First Temple . . . ," in *A History of the Jewish People,* ed. Haim Hillel ben Sasson (Cambridge MA: Harvard University, 1976) 128; and John Bright, *A History of Israel* (Philedelphia: Westminster, 1959) 237. Siegfried Herrmann, *A History of Israel in Old Testament Times* (Philadelphia: Fortress, 1975) 229, gives a cautious assent to the majority view.

Amos to a courageous simpleton.[2] Wilhelm Nowack avoids the issue by simply accepting Amos's own self-deprecating statement about being "taken from behind the flock," a position that comes directly from St. Augustine.[3] There is, in short, very little concerning Amos that has not been said, resaid, and gainsaid.

When one ventures to suggest a new departure for the study of Amos, one is aware of the danger of simply trying to produce a novelty. But if Amos is "one of the most important, if not *the* most important prophet of the Old Testament,"[4] one cannot forbear trying.

The present study is the result of fifteen years of work and thought during which the conviction has grown in me that much previous Amos scholarship has remained too faithful to the traditional Augustinian assumption that Amos was a simple Judean shepherd. Though this naive view of Amos has increasingly been challenged,[5] no one has collected the separate challenges and followed them to their logical conclusion. Doing so, one finds—

---

[2]Artur Weiser, *Die Profetie von Amos*, BZAW 53 (Giessen: Topelmann, 1929); Haran, "Rise and Decline," 273. They seem to follow C. H. Toy, "The Judgment of Foreign Peoples in Amos 1:3–2:3," JBL 25 (1906): 25-28, whose Amos does not rise above the "narrowly national." William A. Irwin, "The Thinking of Amos," AJSL 49 (1933): 102-14.

[3]Wilhelm Nowack, *Die Kleine Profeten*, 2nd ed. (Göttingen: Vandenhoeck und Rupprecht, 1903) 164. A. Neher, *Amos. Contribution a l'étude du prophetisme* (Paris: Vrin, 1950) 17, explains that many important prophets came from humble origins. so no one was surprised at Amos's. The idea that Amos was an eloquent peasant goes back to Augustine, "Christian Instruction," *The Fathers of the Church*, vol. 4: *Augustine*, ed. Roy Joseph Defarrari (New York: Cima, 1947) 187, also cited in James Kugel, *The Idea of Biblical Poetry* (New Haven CT: Yale University Press, 1981) 161. Cf. TB *Ned* 38A and Targum ad loc. with the suggestion that Amos was wealthy.

[4]Richard S. Cripps, *A Critical and Exegetical Commentary on the Book of Amos* (London: SPCK, [2]1955, [1]1929) xl, italics in original. Similar encomia from early exegetes are cited by E. Day and W. Chapin, "Is the Book of Amos Post-Exilic?" AJSL 18 (1901/1902): 65. The acme of Amos adulation is probably Robert H. Pfeiffer's presidential address to the SBL, "Facts and Faith in Biblical History," JBL 70 (1951): 2.

[5]By scholars as various as Barton, Blenkinsopp, Kapelrud, Mays, Silver, and Vesco—see bibliography. Harold Louis Ginsberg, *The Israelian Heritage of Judaism* (New York: Jewish Theological Seminary, 1982) 2, writes that Amos contains a "veritable mine of information on Israelian [Northern Kingdom] beliefs and practices." Not what one would expect from a Judean shepherd, but for all these commentators Amos is still a Judean if not a shepherd.

as Voltaire might have put it—that Amos was not simple, was not a shepherd, and was not even a Judean. Of these three suggestions, the last is surely the most novel.

Amos's Judean origin is almost universally taken for granted. The handful of people who have questioned it[6] has created scarcely more than a ripple on the great tide of tradition. Certainly, no study has been written that begins with the idea that Amos was a native of the Northern Kingdom. But support for just such a position can be found both inside and outside the text. Using evidence that has been overlooked or minimized by the fashionable schools of form and redaction criticism, we will try to reconstruct a picture of the man and his times. The present work represents a return to history-based criticism for the reason that the past forty years have given us a much clearer picture of biblical Israel than we had before. (See, for example, the new histories by John Hayes and J. Maxwell Miller and by Haim Ben Sasson, cited in the bibliography.)

2.

During the long centuries in which biblical study was largely a form of worship undertaken by those with strictly theological agendas, no serious efforts were made to place Amos within his historical context. For example, David Kimchi (or Qimḥi, popularly called "RaDaK," ca. 1160–1235) locates Amos's hometown, Tekoa, in the Northern Kingdom[7] but in his next remark moves on to another subject, giving no evidence for his remarkable assertion, much less exploring any consequences that might flow from it.

Reasons for this sort of summary treatment originate with Augustine, who rhapsodized on the sublimity of Amos's poetry, coming as it did—or so he thought—from a crude, untutored shepherd. The view that prophets are unwilling, even unwitting, recipients of God's word, having as little to do with what they themselves say as a scroll might with what is written upon it, has had the lion's share of proponents from Augustine's time even until today.[8]

---

[6]For a fuller discussion see ch. 2 below, or my "A Northern Amos Revisited: Two Philological Suggestions," *Hebrew Studies* 15 (1977): 132-45.

[7]*Miqra' ot G'dolot* ad loc. Amos 1:1.

[8]Augustine asserted that "not by human effort were those words devised." Day and Chapin, "Post-Exilic," 66, feel Amos's words would have been "marvelous" for a city dweller, impossible for a rustic.

In the modern period of critical scholarship as well, the emphasis, following Luther, is more on the message than the messenger because the
message is, ultimately, more important. Besides, we usually know too little about the lives of most prophets to attempt even Plutarchan biography.
Some have speculated that Amos's presumed occupation left him with
nothing else to do except compose poetry.[9] Modern critical schools necessarily splinter biblical books to such a degree that the portion left to the
"original" author is usually too small to provide a sound basis for investigating his personal history, sense of history, or place in history.

Neglect of a prophet's historical context would be excused by most
historians. Siegfried Herrmann laments that

> For conditions in Israel and Judah during this period (845–745), how-
> ever, we are rather badly informed. . . . This sparseness . . . is all the
> more regrettable since this is the century of the great "writing proph-
> ets," Amos, Hosea, Isaiah, and Micah, and even including the begin-
> ning of their activity.[10]

It is little wonder, then, that Cripps's 1929 commentary (revised in 1955)
compresses the whole period from Solomon's death to Amos's time into
two pages.

Another reason for this neglect is that modern critical interpretation assumes the text of Amos is a kind of stalagmite that has grown slowly over
several centuries of redactional activity. The majority agree that one-third
to one-half of the present text is authentic and original Amos with, perhaps, another fifth added by the prophet after his brief career and the rest
by later disciples or scribes. If this were true, we should indeed be ill-ad-
vised to seek for the history underlying Amos.

To these scholars I would oppose Spinoza's keen observation (on Hosea) that the buffeting of history tends to reduce the prophetic corpus.[11]
David Noel Freedman and Francis I. Andersen assert[12] that Amos's impassioned remarks were collected shortly after a single, electrifying ap-

---

[9]Cripps, *Amos,* 3-5.

[10]Herrmann, *History,* 227.

[11]Baruch Spinoza, *A Theologico-Political Treatise* (New York: Dover, 1951)
148ff.

[12]Francis I. Andersen and David Noel Freedman, *Hosea. A New Translation
with Introduction and Commentary,* AB 24 (Garden City NY: Doubleday, 1980)
147.

pearance, thus protecting the text from much of the later editorial activity that, admittedly, befell other prophetic books—for example, Micah, Isaiah, and even Hosea.

More recently Robert Coote writes that "we cannot expect the few facts available to provide a definitive picture of . . . events."[13] He is here discussing the oracles of Amos, but I hope to show that there is enough information available to clarify much contemporary history, and clear hints in Amos that suggest the prophet knew it rather well. Amos was no simple Judean shepherd but, I will argue, a well-informed native Northerner who, until his fateful prophecy, was a middle-level employee (see below, chapter 4) of the very regime he so violently rebuked.

Integrating insights from sociology, history, and philology, I propose further that Amos

1. had entree into Samarian* society on levels no Southerner, much less an itinerant shepherd, could have had;
2. had sufficient social standing to command an audience; and
3. wrote or was recorded in a dialect of Hebrew peculiar to the Northern Kingdom.

This study is not a verse-by-verse commentary. Rather, it attempts a holistic reconstruction of the Book of Amos, the times that produced it, and the man who wrote it.

I begin with an attempt to refurbish the history of the century preceding Amos's career. There are more than a "few facts available" and we need to know them as well as Amos presumably did. Sections devoted to the problem of Amos's origin (chapter 3), his profession(s) (chapter 4), his own Northern Kingdom "sociology" (chapter 5), the question of the book's organization and authenticity (chapter 6), and, finally, its language and dialect (chapter 7) follow.

3.

Before proceeding, I should identify some underlying methodological assumptions. First, while admitting there can be no proof that what we have is Amos's ipsissima verba, I nonetheless pay particular attention to his vo-

---

[13]Robert Coote, *Amos among the Prophets* (Philadelphia: Fortress, 1981) 21.

*I prefer Samarian to "Samaritan" because of the underlying Hebrew *shomron* and because of the inevitable association of Samaritans with the New Testament "Good Samaritan."

cabulary. If "Amos" did not write Amos, then others did, but either way
the author(s) was concerned with the meaning of the text. I assume they
chose words carefully.

Following the school of Whorf, Sapir, Ullmann, Bloomfield, and
Goodman,[14] I believe that a "natural language" has no synonyms.[15] This
means that each word has some nuances not found in any other, no matter
how closely related the two might be. So Amos's choice of vocabulary is
very important here as elsewhere in Scripture: compare Psalm 92:10 with
Ugaritic Text 68:8.[16] If "poetic requirements" do not override theological
ones, Amos will use just those words that best convey his intentions. For
example, in chapter 3 I unpack the nuances in the phrase לֵךְ בְּרַח לְךָ (Amos
7:12), "exile yourself," and the word קֶשֶׁר (7:10), "treason." Someone,
surely, thought that just these words and no others were appropriate to de-
scribe the nature of Amos's actions as seen by the Northern regime and its
reaction to them.

Second, as previously indicated, I think Amos's words were collected, perhaps written down, shortly after they were spoken, thus making
most suggestions for "redaction" superfluous. My insistence on the essential authenticity of the whole text requires a reevaluation of, among other
passages, Amos 9:8ff., almost universally believed to be post-586 B.C.E.
Chapters 2 and 6 indicate why these verses may be authentic.

Third, I presume that one man named Amos wrote the Book of Amos.
This is not a tautology since it is conceivable that a Southerner speaking
in the North might employ a Northern scribe to record his words. The words

---

[14]The fathers of "semantic field study," from which this assumption comes,
are Jost Trier and Ferdinand de Saussure. Others include Edward Sapir, *Language*
(New York: Harcourt, 1949, [1]1921) 213, who observes that a single language can
belong to distinct cultural spheres, and Nelson Goodman, "On Some Differences
about Meaning," in *Philosophy and Analysis,* ed. M. Macdonald (New York:
Philosophical Library, 1954) 63.

[15]Here is Goodman's definition of synonyms.

. . . two terms are synonymous if and only if . . . (b) each compound
term constructed by combining certain words with either of the terms in
question applies to exactly the same objects as the compound term constructed by combining the same words in the same way with the other of
the terms in question. ("On Some Differences," 63-64.)

[16]William Foxwell Albright, *Yahweh and the Gods of Canaan* (Garden City
NY: Doubleday, 1969) 8, terms Ps 92:10's version "theologically superior" but
gives no reasons for or explanation of this judgment.

of Amos, however, contain so many strange spellings,[17] forms, and preferences that the whole gives the impression—to me, anyway—that it is an original product, basically unchanged in transcription or transmission.

Given the speculative nature of some of these ideas, it is probably too much to expect the results will be immediately accepted. I would be satisfied, however, if I establish a case for my thesis sufficiently plausible that the scholarly community is moved to reconsider the subject seriously.

Readers less familiar with the subject might wish at first to skip chapters 3 and 4, and read the chapter on sociology after the one on history. It is hoped that whatever order the reader elects, he or she will emerge with a coherent picture of the whole.

4.

Twelve years ago I stood upon the hillock of Judean Tekoa gazing out with a "wild surmise." Even then I felt that if Amos had ever stood there, it would have been only after expulsion from his native land. Every step I have taken since has led to the same conclusion.

---

[17]William Rainey Harper, whose Amos commentary was outstanding in its day, suggested that "all the misspellings are textual errors" (*A Critical and Exegetical Commentary on Amos and Hosea,* ICC [Edinburgh: T. & T. Clark, 1905] cxxviii). Such a cavalier attitude toward the text is no longer possible.

Map 2   **The Political Chessboard in Amos's Time***

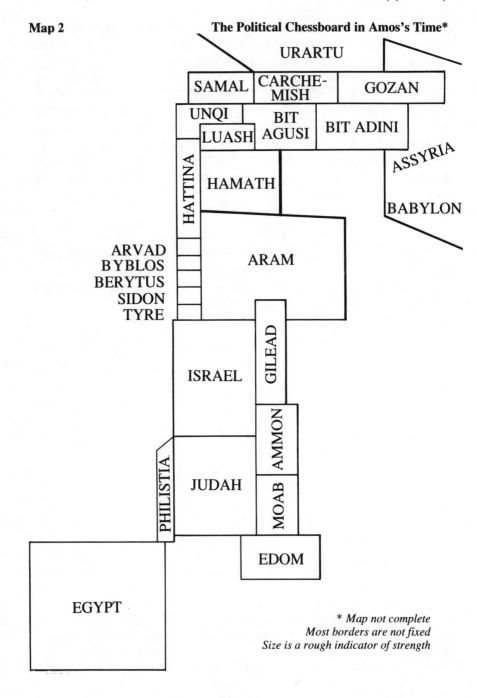

* Map not complete
Most borders are not fixed
Size is a rough indicator of strength

2

History and Politics of Amos's Time

You forget the importance of being in a party of three on the European chessboard. —Bismarck

Political "chess" in the ninth and eighth pre-Christian centuries was probably more complicated than in Bismarck's time. In any case, it is harder for us to replay. There were more countries ("chess pieces") having wildly unequal values, and even the "chessboard"—the physical geography of the Middle East—is not the same now as it was then (see map 2). If we wish to understand exactly what happened, we have first to refurbish the board, that is, reconstruct the physiognomy of the land, before we can gauge its effects, both major and minor, on the players.

To extend the metaphor, the rules of chess are agreed upon; the facts of ancient history are not. Basic tools such as chronology remain somewhat blunted by scholarly disagreement and it is just here that we need the greatest amount of precision.[1] While we can be sure of certain dates such

---

[1] I follow the chronology of Edwin R. Thiele, *The Mysterious Numbers of the Hebrew Kings,* 3rd ed. (Chicago: University of Chicago Press, 1963), and updated as *A Chronology of the Hebrew Kings* (Grand Rapids MI: Zondervan, 1983). Thiele has done much to illuminate this period, but he confesses (p. 39) that the period 798–723 B.C.E. is "most perplexing."

as the eclipse of the sun in 763 B.C.E.,[2] and fairly confident that Amos's career unfolded within a few years of that widely noted event, other important dates and events are controverted.

Combinations of dates and events, like individual chess positions, are capable of many interpretations, hence many continuations. Where dates cannot be accurately fixed—for example, the earthquake of Amos 1:1[3]— possibilities multiply exponentially. Taking another example, the Zakir inscription is dated to about 780 B.C.E. by ANET, but to 755—a whole generation later—by DOTT.[4] The entire historical reconstruction upon which we are embarked could be said to depend on which of these dates is the more accurate. But the same might be said about many of the facts whose place has not been definitely settled. No wonder, then, that previous studies of Amos have been chary of connecting him with the events of his time.

But taking Amos out of his historicopolitical context is like removing a knight from the board before deducing its function. We may infer certain things from its size and shape, but we will not learn half of what there is to know. For example, the question of Amos's relation to sycamores (*Ficus sycomorus*) has been argued for over 100 years. I hope to provide new insights here (below, pages 47-50). For the time being, let me assert that this facet of his life offers an important key to his place in society, a place that was much higher than our traditions remember.

It is true that we stand a goodly distance in time away from the events we wish to examine: much has been lost or forgotten. But despite the hazards, we surely have enough material to justify making an attempt to reconstruct the history of Amos's time. We have, in addition, a duty to do just that.

However much the words of Amos might mean to us today, his message was originally given to and for an audience of his own time. Amos

---

[2]Cf. W. M. Feldman, *Rabbinic Mathematics and Astronomy* (New York: Hermon, !978, ¹1931) 130, who dates it to 9 February 784. No one follows Feldman, perhaps because Amos's allusion to an eclipse loses value the farther back in history the event is. Still, I note that 784 was right before the death of Adad-nirari III, but this was something the rabbis of 1,000 years later probably were not aware of.

[3]This is based on Yigael Yadin's work at Hazor, *Hazor II. An Account of the Second Season of Excavations* (Jerusalem: Magnes, 1960) 36. Shlomo Yeivin, "The Age of Monarchies," in WHJP, 162ff., puts it in 749.

[4]ANET; DOTT 242.

could entertain no hope he would be heeded if his audience did not know what he was talking about, that is, if he and they did not share at least some knowledge of Israel's situation. Our first task, then, is to ask the Book of Amos to share some of that knowledge with us.

Even as a united monarchy, Israel faced the timeless problem of what sorts of relations to establish with neighboring tribes and countries. In the heady days of David, Israelite "foreign policy" seems to have been un-diluted imperialism, while in the broad days that followed, Solomon's policy was one of consolidation and conciliation supported by far-reaching commercial alliances. His marriage to Pharaoh's daughter secured the southern border, for a time anyway,[5] and he enjoyed mutually beneficial relations with Phoenicia.

Nestled between the dry transjordanian plateau and the sea, Israel was in a splendid position to share in the benefits from the trade that connected Egypt, Anatolia, and Mesopotamia. Its coast had some usable ports and, more important, both the Via Maris and the King's Highway passed through territory Israel often claimed and sometimes possessed.

When the kingdom split, policy problems multiplied. It was the northern half, Israel, that fell heir to the Phoenician alliance--most notably symbolized by the marriage of Ahab to Jezebel, the daughter of Ittoba'al (Ethba'al) of Tyre. Ahab's development of Samaria, his father's capital, made that city both a fortress and a showplace. Long after Omri's brief dynasty fell, Israel was still know as *bit Humri* ("the house of Omri"), an ironic testament to its former strength.[6] Of the four Omride kings, the strongest and best was certainly Omri's son and successor, Ahab (874/3–851).

Much of what Ahab built was destroyed and the remains borrowed by later builders. Nevertheless, enough remains at Samaria and Megiddo[7] to

---

[5]Shishak's attack on Israel in 925, five years after Solomon's death (1 Kgs 14:25) may be reflected in Amos 5:19—see below p. 19.

[6]Sargon's Annals, ANET 285. Stephanie Page, "A Stela of Adad-nirari III and Nirgal-eres from Tell al Rumiah," *Iraq* 30 (1968): 142ff., suggests *bit Humri* might be only a variant—the Adad-nirari stele from Tell Rimah employs "Samerina" for Israel—but even so, more than a century had passed since the last Omride king. Subsequent kings would be known to the Assyrians.

[7]"Solomon's stables" at Megiddo are now credited to Ahab. Y. Yadin, "New Light on Solomon's Megiddo," BA 23 (1960): 62-68. This is seconded by Kathleen Kenyon, *Royal Cities of the Old Testament* (New York: Schocken, 1971) 58-59, with further references there. More is at stake here than simply being courteous about assigning credit where due.

show that the former was, in its day, the most impressive city in the Northern Kingdom. Its wealth can be judged by the famous ivories and ostraca found there,[8] its strength by the surviving masonry. The town walls were thirty-three feet thick on the hill's weakest side and of a quality not surpassed until Herod's day.[9]

The shift to Samaria from Tirzah, Omri's first capital, has provoked much discussion. Both cities were well placed to interdict the two longitudinal trade routes, and Tirzah was more centrally located. But Kathleen Kenyon calls it a "backwater"[10] and, indeed, most observers extol the advantages of Samaria. Samaria offered greater defensibility because of its strategic location, an isolated hill with an unobstructed 360-degree view that, on the west, touched the Mediterranean. Perhaps most important, Samaria had no previous connection with key events or persons in Israelite history.

This is important to Albrecht Alt, for one, who feels the move reflects Omri's emulation of David's choice, Jerusalem, and for the same purpose—a neutral site that could be passed on to Omri's heirs. Martin Noth suggests Omri might have been a Canaanite and hence interested in creating a state-within-a-state to resist the tide of Israelite-Yahwist influence.[11] This idea certainly explains the high level of tolerance for, or encouragement of, non-Yahwistic religion in the Northern Kingdom, a fact that will be of great importance to this study of Amos.

We know something of what went on in the city, too. The Bible condemns Ahab for permitting baalism (see Ho 8:5; 1 Kgs 16:32). Part of this,

---

[8]There are some 102 Samaria Ostraca dating from the reign of Jeroboam II and coming from an area (crown lands?) within ten miles of the capital. See ANET 321, and a fuller presentation in Yohanan Aharoni, *The Land of the Bible* (Philadelphia: Westminster, 1967) 315-27.

[9]Thus Kathleen Kenyon, *The Bible and Recent Archaeology* (Atlanta: John Knox, 1978) 68.

[10]Kenyon, *Royal Cities,* 72.

[11]An easily accessible version of the thesis is "The Monarchy in the Kingdoms of Israel and Judah," in *Essays on Old Testament History and Religion* (Garden City NY: Doubleday, 1968) 322-23. Alt postulates that Omri was trying to reestablish the Amarna-age feudalism that Israel's "peasant revolution" (the term is N. K. Gottwald's) had overthrown. This idea makes sense if Noth is correct (e.g., in *The History of Israel,* 2nd ed. [London: A. & C. Black; New York: Harper, 1960] 230 n.1) in thinking Omri and his son were Canaanites. Siegfried Herrmann, *A History of Israel in Old Testament Times* (Philadelphia: Fortress, 1975) 206ff., is a student of Alt's.

no doubt, was to accommodate Jezebel, Ahab's Phoenician wife, but there is some possibility that Israelites (even more than Judeans)[12] either joined in the worship of foreign gods (condemned by Amos) or at least used the calf (not condemned by Amos) to symbolize God in their own worship (not the name *Egelyau* in the Samarian Ostraca), thus engaging in a syncretism which Yahwists would reject. Later I will try to explain why Amos does not reject baalism[13] as he does the worship of other foreign gods in the North.

For the moment we might reflect on the treatment of Ahab elsewhere in the Bible. How strong and important he was may be deduced from the amount of space given him in 1 and 2 Kings. Kings's editors make much of Ahab's moral turpitude, but the good that he did was not entirely interred with his bones. Later rabbinic tradition, freer from the necessity of pillorying the North, remembers Ahab as a man who, but for the Naboth incident, would have had more good deeds to his credit than bad ones.[14] Even the account in Kings gives us a picture of a man with considerable skills, both as a diplomat and as a military leader. At this point we can begin a serious reconstruction of the 100-year period preceding Amos.

Ahab's wealth and power were so great that he may well have seen himself as the new Solomon, ushering in a period of prosperity, if not of peace, for the entire area, from the ladder of Tyre to the river of Egypt. One has to wonder whether, indeed, he was the chief architect of the south Syrian coalition that successfully withstood Assyria in the mid-ninth century. To judge from Assyrian records, Ben-hadad of Aram had the bigger army,[15] but for just that reason the Syrian king might have had an exag-

---

[12]E.g., Ahaz's (732-716) importation of an altar from Damascus; Amaziah's importation of Edomite gods. The latter is discussed below, p. 23.

[13]This has been noticed before. Hans Walter Wolff, *Joel and Amos,* Hermeneia (Philadelphia: Fortress, 1977) 331-32, finds allusions to Baal worship in Amos 8:14. Yehezkel Kaufmann, on the other hand, *The Religion of Israel. From Its Beginnings to the Babylonian Exile,* trans. M. Greenberg (Chicago: University of Chicago Press, 1960) 143 and 365, finds the sole referent to Israelite idolatry (Amos 5:26) "incidental." Kaufmann says Amos was simply more interested in "social" than "religious" crimes, but the distinction is specious. For our discussion, see below, pp. 56-58.

[14]TB Baba Kama 17a, cited by Henri Guttel in EJ 2:439.

[15]See ANET 278-79 for the Assyrian account.

gerated sense of his own strength: he attacked Israel even while Assyria was on the march.[16]

Again like Solomon, Ahab was wise enough to pardon Ben-hadad's repeated incursions despite the Syrian's near success in overrunning Samaria itself. When Ahab outgeneraled his adversary and captured him (1 Kgs 20:26-34), the Israelite ruler contented himself with extracting promises to return the Gilead and grant commercial concessions in Damascus. These promises were not kept. Furthermore, Ahab's generosity was repaid by treachery.

In the next battle (853), Ben-hadad instructed his soldiers to seek out and kill Ahab; this they succeeded in doing. The anti-Assyrian coalition survived until 841, but I have the feeling that desperation in the face of Assyria's mounting strength rather than some vision of regional solidarity motivated the confederates. Moreover, just then Assyria was having serious problems with Babylon and Urartu (Ararat).[17] Though the empire made two westward forays (849, 845) it was another twelve years before the Assyrians could bring their full weight to bear there. When they did, the coalition crumbled.

The political chessboard of the Near East in the ninth century B.C.E. had a cast to it that Bismarck would have recognized. Every white square was surrounded by black squares and vice versa. As in nineteenth-century Europe, each state desired alliances with countries on the other side of those adjacent to itself.[18] When Edom and Libnah broke free of Judah in 841, the Judeans could not pursue them without either first making alliance with Israel to avoid a two-front war or making alliance with Aram to threaten Israel from the rear.[19] The Aramean alliance would have had the further

---

[16]Menahem Haran, "The Rise and Decline of the Empire of Jeroboam ben Joash," VT 17 (1967): 268, says such action would be "inconceivable" during times when Assyria was strong, but this assumption has no factual basis.

[17]For a good popular presentation, see Boris Piotrovsky, *Urartu* (New York: Cowles, 1969).

[18]This is Raymond Sontag's "theory of odd numbers" applied to the ancient Near East: *European Diplomatic History 1871–1932* (New York: Appleton, 1933). My thanks to K. R. Nilsson, Dickinson College Political Science Department, for the reference and consequently this chapter's epigraph.

[19]Alliance with Russia against Germany was the keystone of France's successful foreign policy during the nineteenth century. In the recent Iran-Iraq war, Iran supported Kurdish separatists who, fighting in northwest Iraq for a homeland of their own, constituted a second front against Iraq.

attraction of providing an ally to face Assyria, which also coveted Edom (and later claimed it).

Imputing this strategem to ancient Near Eastern rulers is not conjecture. Already, after the death of Solomon, Asa of Judah had used it (1 Kgs 15:16ff.), enlisting the Arameans to keep Israel from falling upon and devouring his weaker kingdom. Ahab was more clever. He moved from a position of threatening the weaker Southern Kingdom to one of courting it. By marrying off his daughter (and Jezebel's?),[20] Athaliah, to Jehoram of Judah (853–841), Ahab turned the Southern Kingdom into a catspaw for use against rebellious Moab and, finally, into a junior partner in his attempt forcibly to repossess Gilead from Aram. The attempt cost his life. Even so, had his sons been as diplomatically astute as he was, the dynasty might have survived.

Winning Judea to his side was a political triumph for Ahab because, left to their own devices, the Judeans should naturally have pursued the pro-Aramean policy option for the reasons given above. Israel, too, had more to gain from an alliance with Aram than it could reasonably expect to gain in war. But the fall of the House of Omri and the breakup of the coalition left each country to fend for itself. The new regime in Samaria, as we shall shortly see, painted itself into a diplomatic corner and was left with only one alternative, namely, an alliance with yesterday's prime enemy, Assyria. It may be wondered whether anyone, north or south, would have seen submission to the Assyrian lion as anything more than a necessary expedient. But this lion had sharp claws; for better and for worse, the Assyrian connection became the cornerstone for much foreign policy west of the Jordan. As A. Leo Oppenheim observes,

> all fluctuations in Assyrian military potential beginning with Tiglath-Pileser II (967–935 B.C.), a contemporary of Solomon, are reflected in the political stability of Syria and Palestine.[21]

It is beyond question that when Jehu made the sudden shift to a pro-Assyrian policy, the move saved his newly acquired kingdom.

Probably the most eventful year in Israel's history after the death of Solomon was 841 B.C.E. In that year Shalmaneser III (858–828) divided

---

[20]Was Athaliah the daughter of Ahab? Of Jezebel? Herrmann, *History,* 226 n.8, gives references that espouse several alternative theories. The correct answer, if it can be known, is less important here than the fact of the "alliance."

[21]A. Leo Oppenheim, *Ancient Mesopotamia* (Chicago: University of Chicago Press, 1964) 169.

and conquered the shifting Syrian coalition that had successfully defied
Assyrian arms for seventeen years. His army reached the Mediterranean
Sea. One of the things they did on the way was to destroy Beth-arbel east
of the Jordan (at or near modern Irbid) with such ferocity that its name was
a byword for destruction in Hosea's time (Ho 10:14). Because of the unprecedented Assyrian ferocity, and the fear it must have inspired, it is crit-
ically important to us to determine just where the Assyrians reached the
coast.

Most scholars have identified the spot on the Mediterranean where
Shalmaneser erected his victory stele, Baʻli-raʻsi, with Nahr el-Kelb in
Lebanon, but Michael Astour gives strong evidence to support his contention that Assyria's breakthrough reached the sea at Mt. Carmel.[22] The political implications of this seemingly unimportant controversy amongst
geographers has not been recognized. Let us follow Astour's line.

The south Syrian coalition that had repelled or at least withstood Assyria four times between 853 and 845 was, for all its success, a marriage
of convenience with Irḥuleni of Hamath putting up much of the dowry. Astour believes that Shalmaneser wooed Hamath away from its erstwhile
partners, thus allowing Assyria's weight to fall more heavily on Aram-Da-
mascus, the other major contender for regional hegemony.

Whether or not the other partners knew of Hamath's defection, Ahab's
son and successor Joram (852–841) quickly seized the opportunity provided by the coalition's breakup to enlist his nephew and namesake, the
king of Judah (Jehoram, 848–841), for yet another try at retrieving Gilead.
Notwithstanding its defeat at Aphek,[23] Damascus clung to its transjordanian possessions. Their campaign was unsuccessful—in fact the area remained a coveted and contested prize in Amos's time—and, ultimately,
cost Joram his life as it had claimed the life of his father.

What happened next is recorded in some detail in the Second Book of
Kings and need not be repeated here. But since 2 Kings 1–10 is more interested in religion than politics (not that the two are so neatly separated),
we are obliged to put its story into a wider historicopolitical context.

---

[22]Michael C. Astour, "841 B.C. The First Assyrian Invasion of Israel," JAOS
91 (1971): 383-89. Alfred T. Olmstead was the first to suggest Mt. Carmel and
he is followed by Abraham Malamat (see bibliography, below). *Macmillan Bible
Atlas,* ed. Yahanan Aharoni and Michael Avi-Yonah (New York: Macmillan, 1977)
136, says the Assyrians erected stelae at both places.

[23]Probably to be identified with modern Fiq, east of the Jordan, but the identification is controverted. Haran, "Rise and Decline," 271 n.1, has references.

Briefly, then, Jehu ben-Nimshi—the Israelite army commander at Ramoth Gilead, where he had been confronting the Arameans—drove back in "furious haste" (2 Kgs 9:20) and assassinated Joram, already wounded in battle. Second Kings 9:21 (as also vv. 25-26) pauses to note that this event occurred on the property belonging to the hapless Naboth, the moral lesson being obvious.

If this had been the extent of it, Jehu's actions would not have been without sufficient motivation. Even the timing was not unprecedented.[24] However, his depredations were considerably more widespread. Jehu moved to consolidate power by intimidating the city rulers of Samaria into extirpating the "entire house" of Omri. Second Kings 10:11 insists "Jehu slew all that remained of the house of Ahab . . . until he left him none remaining." Almost as an afterthought, he killed young Ahaziah of Judah (841), who had just succeeded his father on the throne of Judah, and forty-two of his kin who had the misfortune of coming north to visit him just then (2 Kgs 9:16; 10:12-14). Why such murderous thoroughness?

Second Kings 10:16ff. is content to ascribe Jehu's actions to his zeal for God, and why not? Jehu was anti-Omride, and Ahaziah's mother, Athaliah of Israel, was Ahab's daughter. Second Chronicles (22:7ff.), on the other hand, blames the young king's death on his mother's influencing him to pursue the alliance with Israel. In this case, it seems to me that, religion and politics notwithstanding, Jehu likely had compelling military reasons for his actions.

On the front line, Jehu could see that much of Israel's strength was committed against the Arameans in a war that could not be won, but might be lost. If 2 Kings 10:32 is properly sited, Israel was already losing. Worse, whatever forces remained would be insufficient to oppose the Assyrians if they chose to move in strength across the Jordan south of his position, which they shortly did. Worse yet, if the Arameans made a separate peace, as the Hamathites had, the same Assyrian ferocity that had recently levelled Beth-arbel would fall fully on Israel. This had to be prevented.

It is possible, too, that the forty-two Southern "princes" were a delegation from Judah's pro-Aramean faction who wanted Ahaziah to withdraw from the battle against Aram so Aram might be freer to oppose Assyria

---

[24]Wounded or sick kings are notoriously vulnerable. Ben-hádad (Adad-idri of the anti-Assyrian coalition) was hastened to his death by Hazael acting upon the "advice" of Elisha. Was this some sort of revenge for Ahab or just a clever move to destabilize the regime in Damascus? In any case, that is what resulted.

and thus offer indirect support for Judah's designs to repossess Edom. Beside every black square is a white square. . . .

(If this explanation is at all plausible, it could shed some light on the famous enigma of 2 Kings 2:23-25, the story of Elisha and the *forty-two* boys torn up by she-bears. [Were these *Ursus arctorus syriacus*? The text does not specify, but see below, page 19.] Elisha was on friendly terms with the Judean ruling house, but like Elijah, his teacher and Jehu's patron saint, he was anti-Aramean. Does the story, then, reflect the prophet's opposition to any defection by the Judeans?)

In any event, to avoid catastrophe, Jehu took the reins of government into his own hands. This may have placated the Assyrians who stood on his doorstep,[25] but it hardly solved all his problems. Damascus still stood and there were, doubtless, those in Israel (and more in Judah) who were pro-Aramean. These elements would oppose cooperation with Assyria, but it was too late to go back to the status quo ante.

At one blow, Jehu had destroyed the old alliance between Phoenicia and Israel, angered many more in Judah by murdering its king and, I surmise, supporting that king's mother's seizure of the throne,[26] and, lest it be overlooked, estranged many of his own countrymen still loyal to the decapitated house of Omri.

All of this would seriously limit his foreign policy options. His radical solution, as we know from the celebrated Black Obelisk, was to enter into a vassal treaty with the new star of the East. If the Assyrians were at Mt. Carmel, he wouldn't have had far to go to pay his respects. Whether or not Jehu, or any of his advisors, really wished to bow to Assyria, it was the best, perhaps the only, foreign policy Israel could have chosen.[27]

---

[25]More so if Astour, "841 B.C.E.," 387, is right in proposing that Joram of Israel was wounded in battle versus the Assyrians, not the Arameans as the Bible remembers it. Keith Schoville thinks the oracles against Gath, Tyre, and Edom were composed in reference to the events of 841, "A Note on the Oracles of Amos against Gath, Tyre, and Edom," VTSup 26 (1974): 55-63.

[26]Even though Jehu killed Jezebel and Ahaziah (her mother and her son?), Athaliah counseled cooperation with the Northern Kingdom (1 Chron 22:1ff.). Perhaps Ahaziah, when he went north and saw how things lay, decided he should side with the "princes" instead. In any case, someone kept Athaliah on the throne of Judah for six years despite a good deal of smoldering opposition.

[27]Alas, as the vassal treaty between Suppiluliumas and Aziras complains, securing protection does not convey knowledge as to which superpower will prevail. ANET 529 lines 33ff.; DOTT 53ff., with illustration.

Of course, one might ask, why have a foreign policy at all? Hosea (7:8-13) criticizes Ephraim for dallying with Egypt and Assyria. Two generations later, Isaiah would rebuke Hezekiah for trusting in alliances and fortresses. No one seems to have noticed that Amos had the same concern.

Where does Amos's homey little remark (5:19) about a man fleeing from a lion and bumping into a bear, then running home and leaning his hand against a wall only to be bitten by a snake, come from? Is it no more than a peasant epigram? And even so, does it not also have political connotations? I think the lion is Assyria (see Ho 5:13-14), the bear is *Ursus arctorus syriacus,* Aram,[28] and the treacherous serpent is Egypt. (Did not Shishak attack Israel almost before Solomon was cold in his grave?) If Amos knew the design of the Egyptian crown and that the word "pharaoh" literally means "great house," then this verse also contains a particularly audacious pun.

To return to the history, Israel is not Switzerland; neutrality would be impossible, so foreign policy would remain a useful art.

The Arameans continued to press southward; even a raid by Assyria (838), doubtless encouraged by their new client, did not stop the advance. Still, the threat of further Assyrian incursions would have required the Arameans to leave some strength of arms at home and so, ultimately, to accept less than a complete victory against Israel and Judah. When Hazael reached Gath[29] in 835, Joash of Judah, the eight-year-old monarch established on the throne by the murder of his grandmother Athaliah, offered a massive bribe (2 Kgs 12:18) that the Arameans prudently accepted. If Jehu's foreign policy could not buy success, it at least saved Judah (!) from a more decisive defeat.

Amos might have been alive as early as 835. If not, his parents or, surely, his grandparents were. The point of these conjectures is that the upheavals of the mid-ninth century B.C.E. were no further back in Amos's time than the Great War is in ours. And since even earlier stories, such as Assyria's furious and then-unprecedented three-year campaign against Bitadini (Beth-eden), were still known in Isaiah's time (Is 37:12 = 2 Kgs

---

[28]That the lion is, or could be, Assyria and the snake Egypt is a commonplace. The Syrian brown bear persisted in the Lebanon into the nineteenth century. Jehuda Feliks, *The Animal World of the Bible* (Tel Aviv: Sinai, 1962) 39; also "Bear" by the same author in EJ 4:355-56.

[29]As with Aphek (above, n. 23) so with Gath: which Gath remains controverted. Benjamin Mazar, "Gath and Gittaim," IEJ 4 (1954): 227-35, is disputed by Rainey and by Kassis (see bibliography).

19:12), how much more so in Amos's? (This is possibly reflected in Amos 1:5—see below.) The Amos whom we will shortly meet was probably born during the reign of Adad-nirari III (810–783), when Assyria began yet another serious push to the West and the old stories, no doubt, were dusted off.

Ancient Near Eastern politics was as treacherous as the great Unqi (Hattina) swamp in northern Syria: the battle was not always to the strong. Scarcely a dozen years after his triumph in the West, Shalmaneser's reign ended in disaster.[30] Assyria was so consumed by internal turmoil that effective control could no longer be maintained. Taking advantage of this weakness, Hazael of Aram and his son Ben-hadad ravaged Israel, as Jehu had bequeathed to his son Jehoahaz (814–798) military forces that would not have made a respectable parade (2 Kgs 13:7, even if the reading of 10,000 infantry is correct). But just when things looked bleakest, Assyria rose again.

Within the first ten years of his reign, Adad-nirari III attacked Damascus twice. He would in time lead four campaigns there, but the first one (806) came just in time to "save" Israel, according to one interpretation of 2 Kings 13:5.[31] In 798 Jehoash (798–782) became king of Israel and, taking advantage of Aram's preoccupation with Assyria, defeated Damascus three times with encouragement from Elisha. Nor was Israel's strength merely sufficient to deal a time-honored stab in the back to its traditional Northern rival.

Amaziah of Judah (796–767) hired a contingent of Israelites for his campaign against Edom. That expedition proved successful, but its longterm results were nothing short of catastrophic. As 2 Chron 25:10ff. reports, the king dismissed the mercenaries before the battle and, presumably disgruntled over being denied a share of the Edomite spoils, the Northern soldiers pillaged Judah on their way home. Having his country's honor to defend, Amaziah had no choice but to challenge Jehoash to war.

If he thought Israel's preoccupation with Damascus would work to his advantage, Amaziah was wrong. Israel promptly defeated Judah on its own soil, at Beth-shemesh, some seventeen miles from Jerusalem, and captured Amaziah. The victors pushed on to the capital, breached its walls, and plundered its temple.

---

[30]Among many others, H. W. F. Saggs, *The Greatness That Was Babylon* (New York: Signet, 1968) 111, chronicles the turbulent end of Shalmaneser's reign.

[31]This is the view of Haran, "Rise and Decline," 267. Scholarly opinion is fairly evenly divided on the identification of Adad-nirari as the savior of Israel.

In retrospect, Amaziah's defeat and capture might have been rationalized as proper punishment for his foolhardiness, but the temple had not been attacked in the seven score years since Solomon built it. Bitterness between North and South must have reached an all-time high, and would not have abated any too soon. This defilement of Jerusalem most likely took place around 792.

Astonishingly, Anderson informs us that the break was only political and Herrmann writes that "the events have no recognizable consequences."[32] But, consider: did not Amaziah return to Judah only in 782? Animosity would have grown with every year of his captivity, nor did it end with his release. These events probably transpired during Amos's lifetime and a twofold importance attaches to them.

First, they help explain why Amos's reference to the "fallen tabernacle of David" (9:11, below, pages 73-74) need not refer to the much-later destruction of 586 and, hence, need not represent an even-later addition to the text of Amos. Second, I suspect that for some time after the battle the amount of traffic of any sort between the Northern Kingdom and the Southern would have been greatly reduced. If the Northerners still made pilgrimages to Beer-sheva, as Amos 5:5 implies, these will have been exceptional, protected perhaps by some unwritten convention.[33]

In light of all this, I fail to understand why previous commentators have simply assumed that Amos-the-Judean came and went in the North as easily as he did around Tekoa.

While Amaziah was hostage in Samaria, the Judeans elevated his son, Azariah (Amos's Uzziah), to the throne. When Jehoash died (782), Jero-

---

[32]Bernhard Anderson, *Understanding the Old Testament*, 4th ed. (Englewood Cliffs NJ: Prentice-Hall, 1986) 286; Herrmann, *History*, 228, probably following Noth (*History*, 237); and William Rainey Harper (*A Critical and Exegetical Commentary on Amos and Hosea*, ICC [Edinburgh: T. & T. Clark, 1905] 9) sees "no hostility" between the North and South in Amos's time. Students of post-Civil War America must find such a suggestion incredible.

[33]Harold Louis Ginsberg, *The Israelian Heritage of Judaism* (New York: Jewish Theological Seminary, 1982) 33, notes that Beer-sheva is important to the North for the Isaac traditions associated with it. Why just the North? But Beer-sheva would be especially holy to Northerners as the place whither Elijah fled the wrath of Ahab (1 Kgs 19:4). After the fall of the Omrides, if not before, it would be a place of pilgrimage. This does not explain why it escapes the punishment Amos predicts for Gilgal and Bethel. Max E. Polley, *Amos and the Davidic Empire* (New York: Oxford University Press, 1989) 105-107, suggests Beer-sheva escapes destruction simply because it is in the South.

boam II, who had been coregent with his father since the battle of Beth-shemesh, released the captive king, perhaps as a gesture of goodwill. But by then the international situation had undergone a dramatic change.

At about the same time that Jeroboam took sole possession of Israel's throne, two important events occurred. First, Adad-nirari III died, leading to a gradual decline in Assyrian power. Worse—at least for the Assyrians—was the accession of Argishti I (780) in Urartu on Assyria's northern frontier. The Urarteans had been menacing Assyria as early as the time of Argishti's father, Menua; now, and for the next forty years, they would possess a strength that would draw Assyria's attention away from the West until the accession of Tiglath-pileser II, about 745.

And where was Egypt? As luck would have it, Egypt's preoccupation with a civil war left it so weakened that it fell victim to an invasion of Egyptianized Nubians. Like a python, the Nubians based on Napata slowly swallowed the greater part of Egypt. There would be no threat to Israel from that quarter. But there would be no help either.

Not that Assyria succumbed all at once. In 775 and again two years later the Assyrians aimed drives toward Damascus. Scholars disagree regarding which side had the best of these encounters, but that Assyria took the initiative says something.[34] Furthermore, Zakur of Luath and Hamath, mindful perhaps of the old silent partnership with Assyria,[35] use the opportunity to attack Aram from the north. In the scramble that ensued, Hamath, Israel, and even Judah gained some ground while Damascus lost. For the moment, hegemony in southern Syria was clearly in the hands of Israel, the Northern Kingdom.

Jeroboam II's forty years on the throne, thirty years as sole ruler (792, 782–753) make him the Northern Kingdom's longest-reigning monarch. He was also the most successful. Scholarly consensus puts Israel's transjordanian successes in the decade 780–770. Amos would very likely have seen the high-water mark of Israelite power (see Amos 6:13) and the prosperity it brought to some in Israel. Subsequently, however, the burden of protracted war would be increasingly felt, aggravated perhaps by the drought and famine to which Amos refers (4:6ff.; 7:1-3).

---

[34]Andre Dupont-Sommer, *Les Arameans* (Paris: Maisonneuve, 1949), thinks Assyria was the stronger; Simon Cohen, "The Political Background of the Words of Amos," HUCA 36 (1965): 158 n.13, disagrees.

[35]Astour, "841 B.C.E.," 384, points out that although he was militarily strong, Adad-nirari III never warred against Hamath.

Amos could see (or God told him) that Northern Kingdom prosperity was tenuous. Due to Jehoash's earlier timidity, Damascus was only down, not out. Judah had been defeated but not subjugated, and the election of Uzziah had been an unlooked-for boon for the South. Uzziah's fifty-two-year rule (792, 782–740) outstripped even Jeroboam II's. (Only evil Manasseh would have a longer reign.[36])

In the first ten years of his rule, Uzziah made military innovations that helped the newly reorganized Judean army acquire considerable territory at the expense of the Philistines, Ammonites, and others. The major part of his success must have occurred after 792 when his father Amaziah was brought to Samaria as a hostage. When Amaziah returned to Judah in 782, he was no longer king.

Second Chronicles 25:14-20 attributes both Amaziah's defeat at Beth-shemesh and his subsequent disfavor to the "worship" of captured Edomite gods. It is more likely that, following Assyrian usage, Amaziah brought Edomite idols to Jerusalem to "thank" them for delivering their own people into his hands.[37] Even so, this would still have outraged the Yahwists, and it was probably people from that group who eventually succeeded in killing the ex-king.[38]

With the murder of the aging Amaziah, then in his seventieth year, the bitterness of Jerusalem's despoliation was finally avenged. Such historians as Hayes and Miller tend to dismiss Chronicles' report of these events because of alleged *tendenz* on the part of its authors, but the recent discovery of Uzziah's tomb, with its warning regarding the occupant, gives us new reason to take Chronicles seriously.[39] At this point (767 B.C.E.) we stand on the eve of Amos's career.

---

[36]Or, if one follows Albright's chronology and lops ten years from Manasseh's reign, Uzziah becomes the longest-reigning monarch in all of Israelite history.

[37]Morton Cogan, *Imperialism and Religion* (Missoula MT: Society of Biblical Literature, 1974) 116-17, says, "against the background of Assyrian practice . . . Amaziah's act is intelligible."

[38]A curious episode and one in which Kings gives more information than Chronicles. Both sources tell us that the murder was the result of a treasonous plot (קֶשֶׁר)—as Americans would say, "an inside job"—because the ex-king fled to Lachish to avoid the fate that nevertheless overtook him there. May we presume that this was not the first time Amaziah was the object of an assassination attempt?

[39]John Hayes and J. Maxwell Miller, *Israelite and Judean History* (Philadelphia: Westminster; London: SCM, 1977) 395, complain that they cannot check the Chronicler's reports. But I find Chronicles can be useful if one allows for its relatively late date and its biases.

Anyone who wishes to integrate Amos into the historical background
must first try to fill the considerable vacuum surrounding the prophet's
personal life. This is difficult, as we have no direct evidence dealing with
his birth date or his age at any time during his career. Nonetheless, evidence exists (below, pages 45-49) that supports my guess that he was already an adult in 767.

The problem is further complicated by our lack of satisfactory information on the duration of Amos's career. Was his a single public decla-
ration, as Julian Morgenstern and others posit?[40] Was he active only during
the two years "before the earthquake" (1:1), as Theophile J. Meek suggested and later retracted?[41] Or was he as durable as, say, Jeremiah?

We know from the superscription that the termini of Amos's career are
Amaziah's death in 767 and the death of Jeroboam in 753 (following E.
R. Thiele). If the well-known eclipse of the sun (June 763) may be inferred
from Amos 8:9, and if Yadin's date for the earthquake (around 760) is correct, the the period 760 plus-or-minus five years is the most likely time
frame for Amos's activities.

It is important to be as precise as possible on this point because many
scholars push the date of Amos's activity down to 738.[42] Those who favor
this late date assume that Assyrian resurgence under Tiglath-pileser III ov-
erlapped with Amos's career, or at least was close enough to cast its shadow
before it.

If Amos were aware of Assyria's growing strength we should have to
read his book in that light. It is necessary, then, to indicate why we may

---

[40]Morgenstern's studies on Amos cover more than twenty years. In "Amos
Studies IV," HUCA 32 (1961): 295-350, he posits a prophetic "career" lasting
only one day. As we will see in ch. 4, this is quite possible. Wolff, *Joel and Amos,*
91 and 124, probably represents a consensus by positing a prophetic career of less
than one year.

[41]Theophile J. Meek, "The Accusative of Time in Amos 1:1," JAOS 61/1
(1941): 63-64, and "Again the Accusative of Time in Amos 1:1," JAOS 61/3
(1941): 190-91.

[42]E.g., Lods, H. Zeydner (1886), J. Valeton (1884), Wardle, Cripps. Robert
Coote, *Amos among the Prophets* (Philadelphia: Fortress, 1981) 20: "the oracles
that can be assigned to the A stage do not name Jeroboam II, and in other ways
they cast doubt on the view that Amos prophesied during his reign," The doubt
is shared by Abraham Malamat, "Amos 1:5 in the Light of the Til Barsip Inscription," BASOR 129 (1953): 25-26, and by Erling Hammerschaimb, *The Book of
Amos* (New York: Schocken, 1970) 11. Voting with the majority are Albright,
Bentzen, S. R. Driver, Eissfeldt, Harper, Kraeling, Lehrmann, Mays, J. M. P.
Smith, G. A. Smith, and Weiser.

be fairly certain that he was not. To begin with, the majority of scholars who see Amos as being active between 760 and 750 also agree that his prophetic career was brief, even ephemeral. (As noted above, Morgenstern restricts it to a single day!)

Against this, those who favor a later date for Amos can muster only scraps of evidence. Their contention rests heavily on Greek versions of Amos 3:9 where "Assyria" is read for TR's "Ashdod."[43] This slender thread will not support so great a weight for three reasons. First, Urartu, as we have seen, was at least as powerful as Assyria during Amos's time, and just as close—but of Urartu there is no mention, either. Second, Assyria was still a friend of the North. Nothing had happened since Jehu's time to annul the vassal treaty. Amos would need more than political astuteness to predict ruin at the hands of Israel's protector, but we may assume that if he had entertained the thought he would have been quick and explicit in giving vent to its dangers: Hosea was. The unnamed "it" which is to be the instrument of God's punishment of the nations in the oracles cannot refer to Assyria, as some suppose.[44] A prophet who didn't balk at predicting the death of his own king would not hesitate to name Assyria if that were his intention. Third, the mention of Ashdod, taken by Uzziah (according to 2 Chron 26:6), might also be a foreshadowing of Judah's resurgence. But Ashdod was an important port city on the way to Egypt, from the Amarna period to Nehemiah's time. As the verse stands, it is an a fortiori expression, the mirror image of Jesus' "not a jot, not even a tittle . . . " (Matt 5:18).

The other piece of evidence that allegedly points to a late date is the enigmatic *Calneh* of Amos 6:2. Some read "Kullani" here[45] and, since

---

[43]Hammerschaimb, *Amos,* 139. Coote, *Amos,* 21, though accepting the majority who deny the validity of LXX's reading, nonetheless says Assyria's rise was "so imminent that it is taken for granted." Similarly, W. Robertson Smith, *The Prophets of Israel and Their Place in History* (New York: Appleton, 1892) 39, sees Assyrians hiding in the *goy* of Amos 6:14. Cf. R. Knierim, " 'I will not cause it to return' in Amos 1 and 2,'' in G. Coats, ed., *Canon and Authority* (Philadelphia: Fortress, 1977) 163-75. This is attributable to 20/20 hindsight. Considering the importance of Ashdod from the time of Ugarit to that of Nehemiah, its use here is not surprising.

[44]Hammerschaimb, *Amos,* 25, following, though perhaps unwittingly, Hogg.

[45]For Coote, *Amos,* 118, it is a certainty. But can we really base so much on two unsupported emendations and an argument from silence? ANET 282's text is brief and broken. Wolff, *Amos,* 274, is willing to assign the verse to a later time

that city in northern Syria was not destroyed until 738, feel their case is made.

But who says we must regard the cities mentioned in Amos 6 as all destroyed? Using the "Calvinist" logic he shares with Deuteronomy, Amos may be suggesting that if bigger, more-powerful kingdoms are not safe, the Israelites should not assume that their own safety is assured. If, however, *Calneh* refers to Calah, it might indicate that Amos was aware of the magnificient refounding of the city in 879 B.C.E. by Ashur-nasir-pal (883–859).[46] In any case, the demise of the North was already imminent.

On evidence supplied by Tadmor and Thiele,[47] we can be reasonable sure that the Northern Kingdom split into two separate states from 752 to 740. Pekah—the same who allied with Rezin of Damascus against Judah— ruled in Gilead, while the pro-Assyrian Menahem was king in Ephraim only. This may also be safely deduced from Tiglath-pileser's annals.[48] But of Menahem, Pekah, and the son of Jeroboam, Amos apparently knows nothing.[49]

---

on "stylistic grounds," but even if it is original and the reading *Kullani* is correct, the verse might refer to the treaty of 754 by which the city lost its independence. Amos could have known this.

[46]Saggs, *Greatness,* 108. My Amos would be aware of such distant events. James Luther Mays, *Amos,* Old Testament Library (Philadelphia: Westminster, 1970) 157, finds Amos's historical knowledge surprising. Also, Malamat, "Til Barsip," 26. Challenged by Haran, "Rise and Decline," 276-77 n.3. William W. Hallo, "From Qarqar to Carchemish," BASOR 32 (1960): 159, reminds us that Assyrian victories in 857–855 were still used to frighten people 150 years later, 2 Kgs 19:12 or 2 Chron 32:29.

[47]Haim Tadmor, "Azriyau of Yaudi," SH 8 (1961): 249. Thiele, *Chronology,* 46-47, bases this conjecture largely on Ho 5:5, though the same situation seems to be recalled by Is 9:10-17. It is accepted by Francis I. Andersen and David Noel Freedman, *Hosea. A New Translation with Introduction and Commentary,* Anchor Bible 24 (Garden City NY: Doubleday, 1980) 393, and by Mervyn Stiles (private communication) who claims the idea originated with him.

Benjamin Mazar, EJ 15:1,178ff., suggests the Tobiads, whose imposing palace at Iraq el-'Amir is still recognizable, rose at just this time. Ginsburg, *Israelian Heritage,* 89, concurs. If so, they would be leading candidates for kingship in Gilead.

[48]ANET 293.

[49]Why not? An obvious answer is that the Book of Amos was essentially complete before the death of Jeroboam. See Joseph A. Blenkinsopp, *A History of Prophecy in Israel* (Philadelphia: Westminster, 1983) 48. My ch. 6, "Unity and Authenticity," has a fuller discussion.

It is even more noteworthy that while Hosea calls the Northern Kingdom "Ephraim" thirty-six times, Amos does not use this appellation even
once.[50] This is all the more remarkable since Amos does use "Isaac,"
"Jacob," and even "Joseph"[51] as Northern Kingdom appellatives. Can it
be that Amos's career in fact ended before the Northern Kingdom split? It
would seem so. In that case, we must accept the date of 760 plus-or-minus
five years for Amos's prophetic activity and go on to ask how familiar Amos
was with the events of the previous quarter century, from Adad-nirari III's
death to his own time.

What Amos knew is a function of who Amos was, and that is the subject of the next chapter. But few people in Amos's world would have been
unaware that Assyria's decline left hegemony in the West up for grabs. For
all that, Amos himself might be surprised by Tadmor's contention that war-
weakened Assyria actually encouraged Jeroboam against Damascus after
the death of Adad-nirari.[52] But when Jeroboam died, Judah would have
been well equipped to wrest control of southern Syria from Israel, just as
Israel and Hamath had succeeded Damascus a generation earlier.

With the death of Jeroboam's son Zachariah, murdered by the traito-
rous Shallum six months later (still in 753), the Northern Kingdom suddenly ceased to be a serious contender: the Jehu dynasty had come to an
end.

As Blenkinsopp observes,[53] Amos says nothing about the chaos that
followed Jeroboam's death. The only reasonable explanation for this silence (and that of the myriad anonymous editors who allegedly followed)
is that Amos's career ended before 753 and, as we hope to show in chapter
6, his words were collected quickly enough to resist redaction. At this point,
however, we must shift our attention to a closer examination of Amos the
man: who and what was he?

---

[50]Uses of the name "Ephraim" in the prophets: Hosea, 36t; Isaiah, 12t; Zech-
ariah, 2t; Jeremiah, 11t; Obadiah, 1t; Ezekiel, 4t. Hosea's use exceeds that of all
other prophetic books combined. What made him so keenly aware of Ephraim?

[51]Tadmor, "Azriyau," 240. Ginsberg, *Israelian Heritage,* 33. Professor Nahum Sarna feels no Southerner would use "Joseph" in this way (private communication).

[52]Tadmor's attractive thesis concerning Azriyau has been entirely refuted by
his student Nadav Na'aman in "Sennacherib's 'Letter to God' on His Campaign
to Judah," BASOR 214 (1974): 25-39.

[53]Blenkinsopp, *History of Prophecy,* 93.

3

The Problem of Amos's Origin

Who are you that wanted only to be told what you knew before.
—Walt Whitman

One problem regarding Amos's origin is that few people have seen any problem here. It has been assumed Amos was from Judean Tekoa—the present-day surface ruin lying about twelve miles south of Jerusalem—mentioned in Amos 1:1.[1] Jewish sources that mention Amos (TB Ta'anit 3:3 and Aboth 3:6) are not interested in his birthplace, while Christian exegetes seem to anticipate or follow Luther's view that "both the place and the person are insignificant."[2]

This attitude cannot inform serious scholarship, for as Hans Schmidt observes,

---

[1]The handful of commentators who have tried to place Amos's home in the North is discussed below. Representative of the majority who accept a Southern locus is Wilhelm Rudolph, *Joel-Amos-Obadja-Jona* (Gütersloh: Mohr, 1971) 96, where he says (my translation), "His expulsion alone proves that he is no Northern Israelite."

[2]Martin Luther, *Works* (St. Louis: Concordia, 1975) 18:130. The man would be more noteworthy if he were the father of Isaiah, whom he so obviously influenced. Our research into Hebrew dialect (see ch. 7 below) suggests עָמוֹס and אָמוֹץ could be related and, certainly, the chronology of their careers fits perfectly. The problem would be how to explain why Jewish and Christian tradition so completely forgot the connection.

Almost every one of Amos's words takes on a different ring than formerly thought, if they come from a Judean—a foreigner in Israel—or if they are from a Northern Israelite in his own fatherland who speaks to us. One need only think of the threat against the king.[3]

Schmidt was by no means the first scholar to make this suggestion,[4] but his novel notion, buried in a footnote of an address given to German soldiers at the front during World War I, attracts even less attention today than it did at the time. Those scholars who notice it at all do so dismissively.[5]

Hans Walter Wolff is one of few modern (post-1945) commentators who even notice the earlier suggestions that Amos was not a Judean. Wolff does this apparently because his own reading of Amos—that is, that Judean Tekoa is well connected with an "Edomite" or clan wisdom tradition—benefits from the standard identification of Amos with Judean Tekoa. Hence, he mentions the Northern hypothesis in order to dismiss it for lack of evidence.[6]

Wolff does not indicate what the nature of this evidence might be, but we may begin our investigation of the problem by reviewing the evidence in favor of a Southern origin. Traditions connecting Amos with the South are not nearly so strong as Wolff and others might wish.[7]

The textual evidence allegedly linking Amos with the South is scanty. It consists mainly of three verses (Amos 1:1; 1:2; and 6:1), the authenticity of which are generally questioned, and an uninformed reading of Amos 7:10-17.[8]

---

[3]Hans Schmidt, *Der Prophet Amos* (Tübingen: Mohr, 1917) 5 n.1 (my translation). Sigmund Speier, "Bemerkungen zu Amos," VT 3 (1953): 305-306, adds (my translation), "A Galilean who prophesied the death of a Northern Israelite king would certainly find refuge in Judah."

[4]It goes back to Cyril of Alexandria (5th century C.E.), *Works,* ed. Pusey (Oxford, 1868) 1:368, and Pseudepiphanius, "De Vitis Prophetarum," in J. P. Migne, ed., *Patrologia graeca* 43:393ff.

[5]Budde, Weiser, Nowack. The idea seems to have gone unnoticed outside Germany.

[6]Hans Walter Wolff, *Joel and Amos,* Hermeneia (Philadelphia: Fortress, 1977) 123, "Although the rabbinic and medieval assumption that Amos's home town must be sought in the northern kingdom has indeed been revived in more recent times, there has not been convincing evidence offered in support of it."

[7]Siegfried Wagner, "Überlegungen zur Frage nach den Beziehung des Propheten Amos zum Sudreich," *Theologische Literarzeitung* 96 (1971): 653-70.

[8]See n. 1, above.

Many scholars say these verses are additions to the text or contain emendations. Though I do not subscribe to redactional theories that reduce Amos to an almost sedimentary accretion of layers, 1:1 and 1:2 are thought to be additions even by scholars as cautious as Johannes Lindblom.[9] Charles Isbell[10] cleverly reads with the Septuagint that the *words* of Amos, not Amos the man, were current "among the נֹקְדִים" at Tekoa. Henricus Oort[11] argues against a Southern origin on the basis of the unusual מ in 1:1. The phrase should read בְּנֹקְדֵי־תְקוֹעַ (construct state) if it really means to place Amos among the נֹקְדִים of Tekoa.

Other scholars exhort us to look for a northern Tekoa,[12] and indeed, Gustaf Dalman[13] found one in 1924. Dalman does not, however, comment on its antiquity and Professor Eric Myers, who regularly directs archaeological investigations in the north of Israel, informs me (private communication) that northern Tekoa, like so many other northern cities, shows no sign of habitation before the Late Iron Age. If so, we may conclude it was founded after the ruin of 586, perhaps even in memory of Judean Tekoa. At any rate, we do not presently know of a Northern Kingdom Tekoa

---

[9]Johannes Lindblom, *Prophecy in Ancient Israel* (Philadelphia: Fortress, 1962) 242. Karl Budde, "Zu Text und Auslesung des Buches Amos," JBL 44 (1925): 63-64, is so outraged by the poor syntax of Amos 1:1 that he willingly jettisons both relative clauses as later insertions.

[10]Charles Isbell, "A Note on Amos 1:1," JNES 36 (1977): 213-15.

[11]Henricus Oort, "De Profeet Amos," TT 14 (1880): 121-33. This had already been notived by Calvin, *Commentaries. Minor Prophets* (Grand Rapids MI: Eerdmans, 1950) 2:147ff. Calvin surmised, as have many since, that Amos was a Judean who had been a resident alien in the Northern Kingdom for some years.

[12]Notably the redoubtable Hans Schmidt, "Die Herkunft des Propheten Amos," in *Karl Budde zum siebzigsten Geburtstag,* ed. Karl Marti, BZAW 34 (Giessen: Topelmann, 1920) 158-71. The only contemporaries who doubted the Judean origin were Heinrich Graetz, *Geschichte der Juden* (Leipzig: Leiner, n.d.) 1:403, and Thomas K. Cheyne and J. Sutherland, eds., *Encyclopedia Biblica* (London: Black, 1902) 3:3,888-89; but Graetz's Amos is a Danite and Cheyne's a Negevite. In the modern period, only Salomon Speier, "Bemerkungen zu Amos," VT 3 (1953): 305-306, and Menahem Haran, "Amos," EncJud 2:881 (idem, EM 6:272), have expressed reservations. Robert R. Wilson, *Prophecy and Society in Ancient Israel* (Philadelphia: Fortress, 1980) 267, considers, but finally rejects, the theory of Ephraimite origin, while Gwynne Henton Davies, "Amos— The Prophet of Re-Union," ExpTim 92 (1981): 200, astutely wonders why a Southerner was called to correct the North when Isaiah's career indicates no shortage of problems in the South.

[13]Gustaf Dalman, *Orte und Weg Jesu* (Gütersloh: Bertelsmann, 1924) 209.

during Amos's time. For all that, it is curious that Northern Kingdom Tekoa stands in the same relationship to Northern Kingdom (Zebulunite, Josh 19:10-14) Bethlehem as the two Judean cities bearing those names (JT *Megillah* 1:77a).

If further archaeological investigation were to demonstrate that a northern Tekoa did exist during Amos's time, what some might regard as a major stumbling block to the "Northern hypothesis" would be removed. But we need not wait for such a discovery. The Book of Amos neither says nor implies that Judean Tekoa was Amos's birthplace, only that he was (or his words were) known there.

The earliest connection of Amos with Judean Tekoa that I have found is in Eusebius's *Onomasticon* as transmitted to us by St. Jerome.

Elthece in tribu Judae est hodiaque Thecua uicus in nono ab Aelia miliaria contra medidianam plaqam, de quo fuit Amos profeta, cuius et sepulcrum ibedem ostenditur.[14]	El-thece in the tribe of Judah is today Tekoa which is in the ninth mile south of Aelia [Capitolina = Jerusalem] from whence came Amos the prophet and where his tomb is shown.

The good bishop of Caesarea lived 1,000 years after Amos, and, I think, mistakes Tekoa for Eltekeh of Joshua 21:23. (See Sennacherib's Annals, ANET 287-88.) Jerome's time is later still and, significantly, after Constantine's. The reader will recall that Constantine's mother Helena was the first "tourist" whose trip prompted the finding (or perhaps the founding) of so many holy sites.

Other voices have been raised to dispute the bishop's identification, but none of them nor all together seem to carry his weight. The bulk of medieval Christian and Jewish commentary accepts the Judean locus. The reason for this, I think, is the marvelous morality tale that the traditional association allows.

Here is Amos, a simple Judean shepherd, bearding the mighty king of the North in his den as Moses did Pharaoh, David did Goliath, and Jesus did the elders. The homiletical uses are so obvious that one could hardly

---

[14]E. Klostermann, *Eusebius. Das Onomastikon der biblisches Ortsnamen* (Hildesheim: Olms, 1966) 86-87. My thanks to Prof. Robert Sider of Dickinson College Classics Department for help in translation and research, e.g., John Norman David Kelly, *Jerome. His Life, Writings, and Controversies* (New York: Harper and Row, 1975) 154, criticizes Eusebius's errors and Jerome's failure to correct many of them.

blame pious readers for conveniently forgetting the truth even if they knew it. Of course, not all the ancient or medieval commentators agree with Eusebius.

Rabbi David Kimchi (Qimḥi), as we noted earlier (above, page 3), is one of those who have other ideas about Amos's birthplace. Writing another thousand years after Eusebius, Kimchi asserts (doubtless on the basis of 1 Chron 2:24) that Tekoa was "a great city in [the tribe of] Asher," making Amos, perforce, a Northerner. Most Jewish commentators, however, accept Judean Tekoa as Amos's home.

There is probably a certain amount of partisanship in this since the rabbis—indeed, all of us in the Judaeo-Christian tradition— are unself-conscious heirs of the Judeans, not of the Samaritans. Only in the twentieth century have we come to realize how much Hebrew Scripture is Northern in origin. To us, however, such a division is largely academic. Few people have any feeling for the intense rivalry that estranged the kingdoms from Solomon's death to the fall of Samaria, much less what it means for scholarship and for theology.

Defenders of a Southern Amos point to 1:2, the so-called "motto" of the book, as proof of the prophet's Judean origin because it "locates" God in Jerusalem. It would be easy, at this point, to hide behind the judgment of the many scholars who feel that the verse, like 1:1, is added, and thereby discard two of the main props supporting Southern Amos. But the verse as it stands (if not where it stands) comports very well with a Northern origin for Amos. As we shall see later in this chapter, Amos was accused of "treason." What greater treason could a Northerner perpetrate than to suggest that God was in Jerusalem and that the South would rise again?

In a similar vein, the use of *Zion* in parallel with *Samaria* (6:1) is taken, somehow, to offer support for the traditional view or, at least, to show Amos's fine, Olympian (= Jerusalemite) impartiality in pronouncing pox on both houses of Israel. H. L. Ginsberg[15] simply emends the text and reads ביסף ("in Joseph") as the parallel term. A far more interesting suggestion is John Punnett Peters[16] that "Zion," a word whose meaning is obscure, actually denotes that place (city or sacred mountain) where your God causes

---

[15]Harold Louis Ginsberg, *The Israelian Heritage of Judaism* (New York: Jewish Theological Seminary, 1982) 31.

[16]John Punnett Peters, *The Psalms as Liturgies* (New York: Macmillan, 1922) 210. George Fohrer, "A. Zion-Jerusalem in the Old Testament," TDNT 7:295, says "Samaria is the 'Zion' of the Northern Kingdom," without, however, acknowledging Peters.

his name to dwell. Consequently, for Northerners, it would be perfectly reasonable to use "Zion" as a synonymous parallel with "Samaria," a sacred mountain of the Northern Kingdom. "Sion" of Deuteronomy 4:48 is glossed by "this is Mt. Hermon." An alternate spelling, "Siryon," is found in Psalm 29, known for its Ugaritic parallels. (See chapter 7 below for more.)

In 1763 J. C. Harenburg located Amos's home on Mt. Carmel[17] (because of 1:2?), and for another century that is where the matter rested. The next person to address the problem of Amos's origin was Henricus Oort, who did it twice (first in 1880, see note 11 above). In 1891 Oort returned to the subject,[18] this time arguing that Judean Tekoa be ruled out because Amos was a tender of sycamores and that tree cannot grow at the altitude of Tekoa—2,800 feet above sea level—but only below 1,000 feet. George Adam Smith[19] (and others) refuted Oort by pointing out that Amos's trees need not have been located at Tekoa, a solution that despite its problems (see chapter 4 below) seemed satisfactory. Smith had visited Tekoa; he was particularly enchanted by the environs and opined Tekoa was a perfect place in which to raise sheep and receive visions.

When I visited Tekoa, I found nothing there to change my opinion that if Amos ever saw the place it was only after he fled the wrath of his Northern Kingdom's government. That there have been dissenting voices, mine included, proves nothing, save that it speaks to a certain discomfort with the main line of interpretation. Scholarship, however, has little use for feelings. What is needed is a close examination of facts, and the text of Amos supplies a number of facts pointing to a Northern origin.

After World War I, Hans Schmidt made one more attempt to prove that Amos was a Northerner, this time on lexical grounds. In 1920 he wrote that if Amos were a Southerner, the priest Amaziah should have told him to "return" (שׁוּב) instead of saying לֵךְ בְּרַח לְךָ. The choice of words is

---

[17]J. Harenburg, *Amos Propheta expositus interpretatione nova latina*, cited in William Rainey Harper, *A Critical and Exegetical Commentary on Amos and Hosea*, ICC (Edinburgh: T. & T. Clark, 1905) 3. I have not seen Harenburg's work.

[18]Henricus Oort, "Het Vaterland van Amos," TT 25 (1891): 121-26. Similarly Jehuda Ziv, "Bôgēr Ubôlēs Šikmîm—b'Teqoa?" [Hebrew] BM 28 (1982/1983): 49-53, argues that the phrase is only a figure of speech meaning "simple person."

[19]George Adam Smith, *Amos, Hosea, and Micah,* 2nd ed. (New York: Harper, 1928) 77. See also his *Geography of the Holy Land* (London: Hodder & Stoughton, 1895; Fontana reprint, 1966).

important: William L. Holladay defines שׁוּב as meaning "to return to an assumed place of origin,"[20] a nuance not contained in other Hebrew verbs for flight.[21]

Schmidt's contemporaries remained unconvinced and he did not pursue Amos southward. Had he done so, he might have concluded that, if Amos was not deported, he must have been exiled. This is what the text in fact says. The critical verse, of course, is 7:10. The expulsion order makes use of a phrase composed of two expressions, each of which needs to be examined.

The following table is taken from my study "A Northern Amos Revisited: Two Philological Suggestions."[22] It shows that the verb ברח almost always means "to cross a border or boundary in order to escape jurisdiction to which one is normally subject."[23] We can see from this array of verses that to flee (ברח) is to leave one's accustomed place of residence to avoid prosecution or death at the hands of one's own ruler or government. To say, as Wilhelm Rudolph does, that בָּרַח is essentially synonymous with נוּס is to say, ultimately, that the Bible may be effectively studied in translation. Compare Amos's flight with Joseph's escape (נוּס) from Mrs. Potiphar. Bernard Grossfeld's careful study traces the scholarly discussion of differences between these two terms back to the eighteenth century. He also points out Targumic evidence which indicates that ברח has a more restricted range of meaning than נוּס.[24]

---

[20]Schmidt, "Herkunft des Propheten Amos," 158. William L. Holladay, *The Root SUBH in the Old Testament* (Leiden: Brill, 1958). There are problems inherent in diachronic word studies; they have great value nonetheless.

[21]Rudolph, *Joel-Amos-Obadja-Jona*, 250 n. 12, burkes the question by asserting that words for "flight" are essentially synonymous. Chaim Rabin, "BARIAH," JTS 47 (1946): 38-41, states that ברח means "escape by stealth," which is consistent with my definition of it. J. Gamberoni, ברח, TDOT 2:250, adds the valuable suggestion that ברח often means "evasion of and escape from continuing unpleasant dangerous situations, e.g., tensions and tragedies *within the tribe*" (italics added).

[22]HS 15 (1977): 138.

[23]My definition. Num 24:11, which I deal with in my article (see n. 22, above), contains the only possible exception. Even there, I think the definition holds.

[24]Bernard Grossfeld, "The Relationship between Biblical Hebrew ברח and נוס and Their Corresponding Aramaic Equivalents in the Targum— ערק, אפך, אזל: A Preliminary Study in Aramaic-Hebrew Lexicography," ZAW 91 (1979): 107-23.

Table 1.   בָּרַח "flight," selected uses

| | PERSON | RESIDES IN | "FLEES" | GOES TO |
LOC CIT				
Gen 27:43	Jacob	south	Esau	Paddan-Aram[1]
31:20, 21, 22, 27	Jacob	Paddan-Aram	Laban	Gilead[2]
Exod 2:15	Moses	Egypt	Pharaoh	Midian
14:5	Israel	Egypt	Pharaoh	unspecified[3]
Jdg 9:21	Jotham	Shechem	Abimelech	Beer[4]
11:3	Jephthah	Gilead	his brothers	Tob (Transjordan)
1 Sam 19:12, 18	David	unspecified	Saul	Ramah (Lebanon)
20:1	David	Ramah	Saul	(Jonathan)
21:11(10); 22:17	David	Nob	Saul	Gath
22:20; 23:6	Abiathar	Nob	Saul	Keilah[5]
27:4	David	(Israel)	Saul	Gath
2 Sam 13:34, 37, 38	Absalom	(Jerusalem)	David	Geshur (Transjordan)
15:14; 19:10(9)	David	Jerusalem	Absalom	River Jordan[6]
1 Kgs 2:39	servants of Shimei	Jerusalem	Shimei	Gath[7]
11:17	Hadad	Edom	Solomon	Egypt[8]
11:40	Jeroboam	Israel	Solomon	Egypt[9]

N.B.: Pss 3:1 and 57:1 remember two of David's flights, from Absalom and Saul, respectively. It makes no difference whether or not these are historically accurate, but the consistency of vocabulary rather speaks affirmatively.

*Verse numbers in parentheses indicate EVV numberings variant from that of the Hebrew.
[1]Remembered in Gen 35:1; Ho 12:13.
[2]After some twenty years he is a "permanent resident."
[3]In cases where destination or point of origin are not specified there is a strong presumption that borders are crossed.
[4]Either in Issachar or Moab, the latter as yet unlocated.
[5]In Judean Shephelah, known by 1 Sam 23:13 to be loyal to David.
[6]See 1 Kgs 2:7; he crossed it.
[7]Cf. 2 Sam 4:3.
[8]See also 1 Kgs 12:2.
[9]See also 2 Chron 10:2.

This evaluation may be easily seconded and strengthened by reference to Jonah. Jonah is probably a fiction; but for just that reason we would expect his story to show literarily correct usage of Hebrew terms. And what term describes Jonah's flight? ברח. Had Jonah read Psalm 139:7ff. he might have saved himself the trouble. The psalmist tells us, eloquently, that there is no flight (ברח) from God's jurisdiction—which, of course, is the point of Jonah.

Abraham Malamat's translation of the extradition portion of the Egyptian-Hittite Treaty of 1294 B.C.E. uses בָּרַח.[25] We know from Jeremiah 26:20

---

[25]Abraham Malamat, *Sources for Early Biblical History* (Jerusalem: Academon, 1970) 207.

that one Uriah ben Shemaiah who had fled (ברח) to Egypt was extradited to Israel and killed by Jehoiakim (see note 30 below).

The definition of בָּרַח as "flight to avoid lawful prosecution/jurisdiction" is reinforced by an examination of its immediate context, the phrase לְךָ . . . לְךָ. Translators, no matter which words they choose, generally regard this as an "ethical dative" (GKC 119s), almost a friendly reminder.[26] Indeed, many have wondered at the mildness of Amaziah's reaction, "Go, flee away to the land of Judah" (Amos 7:12).[27] Later we will investigate why Amos was not killed outright or at least imprisoned as was Micaiah under Ahab.

Translators invariably put a comma in the phrase; the "go, flee away" of RSV goes all the way back to the Vulgate's *vide, vadens, fuge.* NJPST has "Seer, off with you to the land of Judah!" thereby dropping part of the phrase even though rabbinic tradition sees the phrase as composed of two serious commands. The Masoretes connect its verbal elements by *Tiphkah* and *Merkhah,* a conjunctive pair. We have already seen how serious is the command to "flee" (ברח); the other part of the phrase is equally serious.

Umberto Cassuto gives several examples, beginning with Genesis 12:1, in which לְךָ . . . לְךָ applies to

(someone or something) who goes alone (or with those who are specially connected with him) and breaks away from the community or group in whose midst he was till that moment.[28]

Abram, the subject of Genesis 12:1, was no criminal fleeing for his life; Amos was. What crime did Amos commit that merited exile from "the community or group in whose midst . . . "— exile to a foreign country? The answer, as the text itself (Amos 7:10) makes clear, is קֶשֶׁר, "treason."

---

[26]This is a situation in which one party warns another of the anger of a third. Even Grossfeld, "Relationship," 108 n.3, sees nothing else here.

[27]Joseph A. Blenkinsopp, *A History of Prophecy in Israel* (Philadelphia: Westminster, 1983) 91, and Wolff, *Joel and Amos,* 310, discuss in detail the possible relationship between Amos and Amaziah.

[28]Umberto Cassuto, *A Commentary on the Book of Genesis,* 2 vols., trans. Israel Abrahams (Jerusalem: Magnes Press, 1961, 1964) 2:311.

Some translate קֶשֶׁר as "conspiracy" (for example, RSV), but there
is no hint of accomplices here, not even a scribe to take notes.[29] Of course,
the power of a prophet to "create calamity" (Lindblom's apt phrase) is
well and widely known: compare Elisha's trip to Damascus (2 Kgs 8:7ff.)
that eventuates in Hazael's murder of old Ben-hadad. But no one refers to
Elisha's act as "treason" because treason can only be action taken against
one's own government (or legitimate foreign suzerain).[30] The following
table is not exhaustive, but it contains two dozen biblical instances in which
this is precisely the case.[31]

From this table we may learn that people committing קֶשֶׁר in the Bible
are most often intimates of those against whom the action is taken. If Amos
were a Judean, he would be the only foreigner ever accused of treason.
This apparent anomaly disappears if we accept Amos as a native Northerner. Those who minimize semantic differences between related words or

---

[29]Harold Henry Rowley, "Was Amos a Nabi?" in *Festschrift für Otto Eissfeldt,*
ed. Johann Fück (Halle an der Salle: Max Niemeyer, 1947) 197, says there is no evidence of companions. This does not seem to have deterred most commentators from
translating the word as though Amos were part of a group. Blenkinsopp, *History of
Prophecy,* 91; Richard S. Cripps, *A Critical and Exegetical Commentary on the Book
of Amos,* rev. ed. (London: SPCK, 1955) 229; Norman H. Snaith, *Amos, Hosea, and
Micah* (London: Epworth, 1946) 125, "plotting." Harper (ICC), assuming Amos is
Judean, understands his behavior as sedition, leading to conspiracy. Gene Tucker,
"Prophetic Authenticity. A Form-Critical Study of Amos 7:10-17," *Interpretation*
27 (1973): 427, "Had he been a citizen of Israel the charge would have been high
treason." But he is, and it is—see below.

[30]2 Kgs 17:4 reports Tiglath-pileser III as jailing Hoshea for contacting Egypt,
and reneging on tribute. Jer 26:20-23 names one Uriah ben Shemaiah as being
fetched back from Egypt, no doubt with Egyptian concurrence, and killed. Esar-
haddon Vassal Treaties, §10, ANET, 535, specifically names prophets as poten-
tial subversives.

[31]There are some twenty texts in which קֶשֶׁר is not so used. My list derives
from Solomon Mandelkern's *Veteris Testamenti Concordantiae Hebraicae atque
Chaldaicae,* 3rd ed. (Tel Aviv: Schocken, 1967) 1,052d-53a. We actually are
dealing with the phrase קֶשֶׁר עַל of which Yair Hoffman, "Did Amos Regard
Himself as a NABI?" VT 27 (1977): 209-12, writes, "This phrase appears in the
Bible in one sense only; it defines a conspiracy in the country itself, committed
by a person legally subordinate to the ruler of that very country" (211). (See A.
Even-Shoshan, *A Concordance of the Old Testament* (Jerusalem: Kiryat Sepher,
1983) 1,039.) Hoffman apparently thinks, as I do, that place-of-birth, not residence, determines one's liege loyalty. Whose tradition was it that caused Joseph
and Mary to return to Bethlehem?

Table 2.   קֶשֶׁר as **"treason"**

LOC CIT	PERPETRATOR(S)	AGAINST
1 Sam 22:8	Saul's Benjamite servants	Saul
22:13	Nobite priesthood	Saul
2 Sam **15:12**	Ahitophel (w/Absalom)	David
15:31	"people" (w/Absalom)	David
1 Kgs 15:27	Baasha, Issachar	Nadav
16:9	Zimri	Elah
16:16	Zimri's servants	Elah
16:20	Zimri's servants	Elah
2 Kgs 9:14	Jehu	Ahab and Ahaziah
10:9	Jehu	Ahab
11:14[1]	Jehoida, Joash	Athaliah
12:21(20)	Joash's servants	Joash
14:19	Jerusalemites	Amaziah
15:10	Shallum	Zechariah
15:15	Shallum	Zechariah
15:25	Pekah	Pekahiah
15:30	Hoshea	Pekah
17:4	Hoshea	Shalmaneser
21:24	Amon's servants	Amon
Jer **11:9**	Judeans, Jerusalemites	God
Ezek **22:25**[2]	princes of city	inhabitants
Neh 4:2(8)	Sanballat, Tobiah, Arabs, Ammonites, and Ashdodites	Nehemiah
2 Chron 24:25	servants of Joash[3]	Joash
24:26	servants of Joash	Joash

*Numbers in **bold** type indicate verses that contain noun forms; those in ***bold italic*** type, verses that contain both verb and noun forms. Verse numbers in parentheses indicate EVV numberings variant from that of the Hebrew.

†English versions routinely translate as "conspire/conspiracy" excepting, e.g. in RSV, in 2 Kgs 11:14 ("Treason! Treason!"); 17:4 ("treachery"); Jer 11:9 ("revolt"); and Neh 4:2 ("plotted").

[1]2 Chron 23:13 is a doublet though with some differences. Both passages have Athaliah exclaiming, קֶשֶׁר קָשֶׁר (the second form is pausal).

[2]Occurrence relegated to margin in, e.g., RSV and TEV.

[3]This is not a doublet of 2 Kgs 12:21 because the genealogies are given. Foreign mothers do not foreign children make; but Chronicles may be trying to suggest a reason for the defection in this case.

political differences between Hebrew kingdoms— the two attitudes seem to go together—need to reconsider what word studies can tell us.

I recognize, of course, that linguistic argument cannot be conclusive. For one thing, we do not know whether Amaziah was using Hebrew with academic precision, or whether we even have his exact words.[32] Robert R. Wilson[33] has no problem with Amaziah's use of חֹזֶה in the same passage. This, he says, was the usual designation for a "prophet" in Judah, as opposed to Israel where the term נָבִיא was usual. Hence, Amaziah gave Amos his "native" title. Ziony Zevit argues further that Amos, a Judean חֹזֶה would ipso facto have no authority to criticize an Israelite king;[34] others suggest Amaziah was simply being sarcastic,[35] a suggestion that makes a lot of sense if Amaziah knew who Amos was, as I suspect. This, in turn, is more likely if Amos were a well-known Northerner than if he were some itinerant Judean shepherd.

The burden of this section has been to suggest that lexical items in Amos 7, namely, בָּרַח, לְךָ . . . לֵךְ, and קֶשֶׁר, combine to suggest that Amos was a native Northerner accused of treasonous prophecy and exiled from his native land—and that those verses usually assumed to prove a Southern origin do no such thing. Whether he was a חֹזֶה or a נָבִיא (or neither) has not been our concern here; that question is addressed in the following chapter. But we also have to ask, what was Amos's customary function in his society? That is, what was he doing during those times—presumably most of his adult life—when he wasn't delivering prophecies? We cannot understand Amos's place in Northern society without knowing more about his profession(s).

---

[32]Ernst Würthwein, "Amos-Studien," ZAW 62 (1950): 19, and Karl Budde, "Zu Text und Auslesung des Buches Amos," JBL 44 (1925): 78, inform us that the high priest's exact words could hardly be known, but that is beside the point. *Someone* wrote Amos with more precision than most previous commentators have noticed.

[33]Wilson, *Prophecy and Society,* 269.

[34]Ziony Zevit, "A Misunderstanding at Bethel," VT 25 (1975): 783-90. This view is criticized by Hoffman in VT 27 and answered by Zevit in VT 29.

[35]Erling Hammerschaimb, *The Book of Amos* (New York: Schocken, 1970) 116. It surprises me that so many scholars do not see significant differences between such related terms as חֹזֶה, רֹעֶה, and נָבִיא.

4

Amos's Occupations

A prophet is not without honor, except in his own land.   —Jesus

One wonders whether Americans 2,500 years from now will remember that Paul Revere was a silversmith, or Europeans recall that Paderewski was a pianist and Kafka worked in an insurance office. Our memories of great people neglect their everyday lives. This quasi-hagiographical remembrance of national heroes might make religious sense, but it is not good scholarship. We need to ascertain what Amos was and not assume we already know it.

John D. W. Watts begins his study of Amos[1] with a section entitled "What Kind of a Prophet Was Amos?" There are, indeed, any number of ways in which to answer such a question, almost all of which assume Amos was some kind of prophet: after all, is Amos not among the prophets? A careful reader will note, however, that I have gone to some lengths to avoid calling Amos a prophet up to this point because it is a major part of my thesis that he was not one. Though he did on at least one occasion exercise a prophetic function, I hope to show that this was far from his usual calling.

My proposition has some ancestry. In 1929 Richard S. Cripps could write, "If not in his lifetime, then after his death he is held to be a prophet."[2]

---

[1]John D. W. Watts, *Vision and Prophecy in Amos* (Grand Rapids MI: Eerdmans, 1958) 1.

[2]Richard S. Cripps, *A Critical and Exegetical Commentary on the Book of Amos,* rev. ed. (London: S.P.C.K., 1955) 9.

Cripps did not recognize how important it is for us to be able to decide between the alternatives. The problem, of course, is that the Book of Amos offers contradictory evidence on the subject.

At one end of the spectrum is Henning Reventlow who argues for an "office" of prophet.[3] This sort of person, following Blenkinsopp, would have automatic access to rulers, his own or foreign (as Elijah had in Damascus).[4] Of course, that might depend on just what kind of prophet Amos was. Würthwein, with a degree of precision to which the present study does not pretend, posits that Amos began as a *Heilsnabi* and changed to an *unheilsprophet* sometime between his second and third visions.[5]

If one differentiates between "cult" and "free" prophets, most scholars identify Amos as a cult prophet.[6] Simon Cohen, however, cleverly punctuates the well-known 7:14 to read, "No! I (am) a true prophet; I am not a בֶּן־נָבִיא"[7]—the latter being seen as a derogatory term for sycophantic prophets of the sort who sent Ahab to his death with promises of victory.

The term בֶּן־נָבִיא has generated its own literature. The anonymous disciples of Elisha were known as בְּנֵי הַנְּבִיאִים, a favorable designation. J. Roy Porter[8] feels this congeries of followers was moribund by 760, so

---

[3]Henning Graf von Reventlow, *Das Amt des Propheten bei Amos* (Göttingen: Vandenhoeck & Ruprecht, 1962). This notion has been criticized by James Muilenberg, "The 'Office' of the Prophet in Ancient Israel," in *The Bible and Modern Scholarship*, ed. J. Philip Hyatt, 74-97 (Nashville: Abingdon, 1965), and by Georg Fohrer, "Remarks on Modern Interpretations of the Prophets," JBL 80 (1961): 311-12.

[4]Joseph A. Blenkinsopp, *A History of Prophecy in Israel* (Philadelphia: Westminster, 1983) 68ff. Jeremiah's is a special case, but at one point he had to send his prophecies in writing via Baruch to King Jehoiakim, since he was barred from the temple precincts (Jer 36:5ff.). (My thanks to Mary Helene Rosenbaum for this observation.) Most scholars do not question the access of prophets to any public officials.

[5]Ernst Würthwein, "Amos-Studien," ZAW 62 (1950: 10-52. This theory of Amos's "conversion" shows an awareness of the inner conflict that, I think, led to his agonized outburst at Bethel.

[6]A cult prophet is one who has a recognized position or function in the faith community's worship or practice. Thus, Arvid S. Kapelrud, *Central Ideas in Amos* (Oslo: Oslo University Press, 1961) 11. Gene Tucker, "Prophetic Authenticity. A Form-Critical Study of Amos 7:10-17," *Interpretation* 27 (1973): 433, disagrees with Kapelrud's assessment.

[7]Simon Cohen, "Amos *was* a Navi," HUCA 32 (1961): 175-78.

[8]J. Roy Porter, "Ben hannevi'îm," JTS 32 (1981): 423-29.

Amos could not have been one. Even so, the group's appellation will have outlived them. Amos might have felt compelled to dissociate himself from a group so recently dissolved, to avoid seeming to trade on their name. Julian Morgenstern's Amos, like mine, "does not regard himself as a prophet at all."[9]

Some[10] see the unnamed "man of God" in 2 Kings 13 as referring to Amos. This is probably not correct, but whether or no, Jewish and Christian traditions are very much in agreement that Amos, unlike Daniel, is among the prophets. If Saul, now much more so Amos? To today's Jews and Christians, there is no doubt that Amos is a prophet. Still we need to ask how matters stood in Amos's own time.

Let us first of all remember that the call to prophesy represented an unwelcome interruption in the normal life of the person called: Jeremiah comes readily to mind. Most of the prophets from Moses onward made some attempt to evade the call: Jonah's strenuous measures, for example, have already been noted (above, page 36). The burden of this study so far has been to show that Amos must be read, as far as possible, against his historical background. Consequently, we must not only remember Jesus' remark about the honor given to prophets but also that even those people who are recognized as prophets probably spent only a fraction of their time prophesying. Here Jeremiah was an exception, not the norm.

The problem is well-nigh intractable. In the verse cited above (Amos 7:14) there is no verb. Scholars— Julian Morgenstern, Harold H. Rowley, and Hans-Joachim Stoebe,[11] to name but three—therefore disagree on

---

[9]Julian Morgenstern, *Amos Studies* (Cincinnati: Hebrew Union College Press, 1941) 174. Like many others, Watts (*Vision and Prophecy,* 8) feels Amos was a substantial citizen who had the role of prophet "thrust upon him." To Georges Farr, "The Language of Amos: Popular or Cultic?" VT 16 (1966): 319, Amos is an "educated layman." Hans-J. Stoebe, "Der Prophet Amos und sein burgerlicher Beruf," *Wort und Dienst* 5 (1957): 160-81, also recognizes in Amos middle-class origins.

[10]The anonymous "man of God" in 1 Kgs 13 has long been identified with Amos, e.g., by Morris Silver, *Prophets and Markets. The Political Economy of Ancient Israel* (Boston: Kluwer, 1983) 160. Cf. James L. Crenshaw, *Prophetic Conflict* (Berlin: de Gruyter, 1971) and Peter Ackroyd, "Amos 7:14," EvT 68 (1956/1957): 94. Certainly the "Deuteronomists" would like us to make this connection, but if it were so, why not name Amos?

[11]James F. Craghan, "The Prophet Amos in Recent Literature," BTB 2 (1972): 243-62, warns us to avoid overdependence on the syntax of one verse, especially when the verse in question does not contain a verb!

whether the remark should be understood as past or present tense. Syntactical questions notwithstanding, virtually the entire weight of popular tradition is in favor of identifying Amos as some sort of prophet.

Admittedly, it is hard to accept Amos's denial when, elsewhere in the book, he does the things that prophets do, speaks the words they speak[12]— even seems to admit his calling in 3:7: "For God does nothing without revealing his secret to his servants the prophets." I discuss this verse in greater detail in chapter 6, "Unity and Authenticity." For now, let me indicate concurrence with the majority view that 3:7 is an addition.[13] Even if it is not, however, 3:8b—"When God speaks, who will not prophesy?"— offers support for Rowley's view, and mine. Rowley's solution[14] to the lack of verb is to translate "I had not chosen the calling of prophet," implying Amos has perforce, only now, become one. The lack of verb allows both Amos's past and present realities to be understood.

The Book of Amos, like that of Isaiah, begins with "words/vision of X (the author)" instead of the more usual "words of God/vision of God." This is not to deny that Amos did indeed perform a prophetic function. But certainly it could not have been the custom for itinerant shepherds to get up and speak during a Northern religious festival as if it were some sort of town meeting. Spiegel's jocular remark about the lack of "freedom of speech" in Samaria misjudges the seriousness of the situation.[15] Amos's antigovernment remarks would be intolerable in most societies, ancient or modern. The real questions are (1) if Amos was not a trained prophet, how did he come by his impassioned eloquence? and (2) how could he command an audience?

Since Jesus' (or even ben Sirach's) time, we refer to "the law and the prophets" as though each of the latter were sainted as soon as he or she could be decently buried. But how soon might a disciple of Jesus have said, "See here, I'm Saint Matthew so you have to pay attention to me"? Even

---

[12]Amos's use of the forms of prophetic speech, however haphazardly, makes me think of Jer 18:18, "the word . . . will not perish for lack of prophets" (JB). Certainly, ordinary citizens were not forbidden to use forms of prophetic speech.

[13]E.g., Heaton, Mays, and Wolff most emphatically. Cf. Gitay and Hammerschaimb.

[14]Rowley concludes that Amos is saying, "I was no prophet, but I am one now" ("Was Amos a Nabi?" in *Festschrift für Otto Eissfeldt,* ed. Johann Fück [Halle an der Salle: Max Niemeyer, 1947] 198).

[15]Shalom Spiegel, "Amos *v* Amaziah," in *The Jewish Expression,* ed. Judah Goldin (New York: Bantam, 1970) 38-65.

if reluctant prophets—and few were not—received grudging attention from those in authority, it is not clear to me that Amos expected that sort of response. The more so if he commanded attention for other reasons.

Conversely, we may assume that the less important Amos was, the easier it would have been to silence or ignore him. A Judean, and a shepherd, would have little standing at the Northern court—even less after Israel's humiliation of Amaziah in 792.[16] But if Amos was a native Northerner and, what is more, a prominent-citizen-turned-social-critic, the situation is quite different. He could neither be safely ignored nor summarily dealt with. Many scholars (Wolff, for example) have remarked on the "m'mildness" of Amaziah's response to Amos, given the prophet's provocation. Expulsion—exile, not deportation—was the best response.

One might combine arguments of Kapelrud and Blenkinsopp to picture a Judean Amos going north because that was "where the action was," and obtaining an audience through some charisma the book does not convey to us. These are weak arguments.[17] King Amaziah's abduction of the Edomite gods, whether or not he worshipped them as Chronicles complains (2 Chron 25:14-16), would have given Judean prophets an object of obloquy much closer to home. Kapelrud is on firmer ground when he directs our attention to Amos's customary, nonprophetic function in society.

Amos does not directly refer to himself as a "shepherd," though he uses the usual term רֹעֶה twice (1:2; 3:12). Instead, we have the *dis legomenon* נֹקֵד (1:1; see also 2 Kgs 3:4), the *hapax legomenon* בּוֹקֵר (7:14), and the expression בּוֹלֵס שִׁקְמִים (7:14). The latter suggests Amos had *something* to do with sycamores; the former two suggest something to do with sheep or small cattle, but what? Cognate terms for נֹקֵד found in Arabic, Babylonian, and Ugaritic (62.VI.53-57) convince Kapelrud and Miloš Bič that Amos was a high cultic official.[18] Wilson,[19] more cautiously, rec-

---

[16]Those writers for whom prophecy may be safely divorced from politics will find this no occasion for comment. But if King Amaziah could be detained for ten years and then sent home like a dog with his tail between his legs, the mighty North will have had no reason to heed one of his subjects.

[17]As mentioned above, ch. 3, n.12, G. Henton Davies, "Amos the Prophet of Re-Union," ExpTim 92 (1981): 196-200, is aware that the South had its own problems.

[18]Miloš Bič's suggestion, "Der Prophet Amos—ein Haepatoskopos?" VT 1 (1951): 293-96, was refuted by André Murtonen, "Amos—ein Hepatoscopos?" VT 2 (1952): 170-71.

[19]Kapelrud, *Central Ideas in Amos,* 68ff.; R. R. Wilson, *Prophecy and Society in Ancient Israel* (Philadelphia: Fortress, 1980) 268.

ognizes Amos as having a position within the Judean (*sic*) establishment, but not necessarily connected with the cult. Indeed, it would be asking much for the term to cross the long frontiers of time and space that separate Ugarit from Israel and retain its precise meaning throughout. Fortunately, there is cognate evidence closer to Amos's time that sheds light on his profession.

San Nicolo points out[20] that NBab *naqidu* occupies an intermediate position between NBab *rabi-buli* and *re'u,* the latter corresponding with Hebrew רֹעֶה. Amos, then, could have been some sort of district supervisor of royal herds since נֹקֵד indicates no ordinary shepherd. The use of the plural נֹקְדִים makes it possible that there were several people, perhaps a guild, with similar responsibilities in different administrative districts. Why a group of these people should cast up in Judean Tekoa remains obscure. If it really is Judean Tekoa, we might suggest that other members of Amos's guild fell into disgrace along with him, even on account of him, and that some emigrated to Tekoa between about 755 and the end of Samarian sovereignty. (In much the same way, we see emigrants congregating in their foreign havens in all periods.)

Admittedly, this is speculation. Craigie, however, has no trouble demonstrating that Ugaritic *nqdm* were

> "sheep managers" responsible for large herds . . . the servants of a king
> . . . liable to the king for service and taxation.[21]

A middle-level position in his government's service would have given Amos the visibility and status requisite to commanding an audience. It might even have made him a personage whom Amaziah could not summarily silence. Furthermore, it implies he had the intelligence and verbal skills to know how to appeal to an audience. (I have more to say on the style of Amos in chapter 7.)

We still must address the problems generated by בּוֹקֵר and בּוֹלֵס שִׁקְמִים. In regard to the former, it may be enough to say the term, if this is the cor-

---

[20]M. San Niccolo, "Materielen zur Viehwirtschaft in den neubabylonischen Tempeln," *Orientalia* n.s. 17 (1948): 273-93, esp. 284ff. Kapelrud, *Central Ideas in Amos,* would certainly accept this.

[21]Peter C. Craigie, "Amos the נֹקֵד in the Light of Ugaritic," *Studies in Religion* 11 (1982): 33.

rect reading,[22] confirms Amos as having something to do with sheep and small cattle, probably in a supervisory capacity. As Craigie puts it,

> Amos was not a simple shepherd. He was in the sheep business, a manager of herds, contributing both wool and meat to the economy.[23]

Since it is not Craigie's purpose to explore Amos's other commercial activities, he does not examine Amos's "fruit farming." It is just here, however, that Amos scholarship has enshrined one of its most engaging misapprehensions.

Commentators assert that a "gasher," "pincher," or "figger" of sycamores denotes a humble station in life, akin to a migrant laborer's. Jehuda Ziv suggests the phrase is simply a figure of speech, perhaps like the American expression "ordinary Joe," connoting, again, one's modest status.[24] The reason for this agreement of the literal with the figurative is that our understanding of the place of sycamores in Israelite economy is seriously flawed.

The use and maintenance of sycamores, from Pliny to modern Israeli experiments, has been detailed by T. J. Wright.[25] But we already knew from 1 Chronicles 27:28 that as early as David's time there was a royal official who oversaw olive and sycamore trees. Cultivation of olives one may understand. What puts sycamores on a par with Palestine's most valuable tree?

Much has been written about its fruit. S. R. Driver complains[26] that sycamore figs are "insipid and woody in taste," more suitable for fodder than for human consumption, and that even for animals the fruit needs prior preparation. The "gasher" or "figger," we are told, has the tiresome job of puncturing the skin of sycamore figs, hastening the ripening process by encouraging the wasps that lay their eggs in them (wasps which, according to Wright, do not occur in Palestine). People involved in such work are

---

[22]It is suggested that בֹּקֵר is an error for נֹקֵד, or vice versa! But בֹּקֵר is a normal Phoenician word for "cattle," as it is in Kilamua/Zincirli Insc., ca. 825, KAI II.31. In ch. 6 I examine more Phoenician influences in Amos.

[23]Craigie, "Amos," 33.

[24]Jehuda Ziv, "Bôqēr Ubôlēs Šikmîm—b'Teqoa?" [Hebrew], BM 28 (1982/1983): 49-53.

[25]T. J. Wright, "Amos and the Sycamore Fig," VT 26 (1976): 362-68.

[26]Samuel R. Driver, with H. C. O. Lanchester, *The Books of Joel and Amos*, 2nd ed. (Cambridge: Cambridge University Press, 1915) 212.

assumed, ipso facto, to be of the lowest class. But what if there is more to sycamore cultivation than that?

We have already mentioned the tree's use in providing fodder. In good years, sycamores fruit six or seven times, while in times of drought (alluded to in Amos 4:6-9), they might be even more valuable because their extensive root system reaches deep into the soil, allowing them to tap ground water and also to prevent erosion.[27] This hardiness is celebrated in Genesis Rabbah 12:6 where the claim is made that sycamore trees live 600 years. If they are cut down, Isaiah 9:8 informs us, their wood is useful in construction. In addition, careful cutting allows them to be "harvested" for timber repeatedly.

Putting all these things together, we can see that the Israelite monarchies would be careful to preserve sycamores lest peasants cut them down for wood and endanger soil retention and crop reserve in time of drought. [As this was being written, Turkish rescue teams are searching for victims of landslides caused by overcutting of trees!] Clearly, the government would need agents whose job was to see that sycamores on crown lands, at least, were not pilfered.

What had Amos to do with all this? I suggest that the association of Hebrew בּוֹלֵס שִׁקְמִים with its Ethiopic cognate takes us in the wrong direction. Wright points out[28] that Palestinian sycamore figs, unlike their East African counterparts, are vegetative parthenocarpic. That is, they do not need gashing in order to ripen. Of course the Alexandrian-Jewish translators of the LXX would not have known that, hence their use of κνίζων συκάμινα ("one who scrapes/scratches/teases sycamores"). The correct solution to the question of Amos's connection with these trees may lie much closer to home.

In chapter 7 we will examine the thorny problem of language and dialect in Amos. One of the points discussed there is the possibility that Ephraimite Hebrew lacked a שׁ.[29] Thus, our בֵּלַשׁ might correspond with בָּלַשׁ or בּוֹלֵס in Targumic Aramaic. We could still read it as "gasher" or

[27]Noted by Ephraim Orni and Elisha Ephrat, *Geography of Israel,* 3rd rev. ed. (Jerusalem: Jewish Theological Seminary, 1973) 46.

[28]Wright, "Amos and the Sycamore," 365.

[29]The observation comes from Alfred Beeston supported by information from Zeev Ben-Hayyim. See bibliography.

"hacker," but we can also connect it with בַּלְשִׁי, "searching tax commissioner,"[30] from בְּלַשׁ.

Admittedly, there is no compelling reason to accept linguistic speculations of this sort on their own, but there is additional reason to believe Amos had a different, and far higher, social and economic standing that Ziv, for example, thinks. In this connection, it is worth remembering that both Targum Onkelos at Amos 1:1 and TB Ned. 38a propose Amos was wealthy, an "owner of herds"—a line followed by many moderns as well. It may be the case, then, that Amos's concern for sycamores is no proof of lower-class status, but the opposite.

The problem with sycamores, as we have seen, is that they do not and cannot grow at the altitude of Judean Tekoa. This is a problem only for those who defend the received notion that Amos was a Judean. Since Oort first raised his objection, defenders of a Judean Amos have countered with several scenarios to explain the situation: *Ficus sycomoros* does grow at Ein Gedi on the Dead Sea and Timnah in the Shephelah (famous also as an area where Judah pastured sheep). Amos, they aver, must have gone to one of those places, taking his flocks with him.[31] This response is logical, but it raises more questions than it answers.

How does a "simple shepherd" come to tend trees so far from his home? If they are his trees, why does he live in Tekoa? If they are not, how doest he obtain leave to graze his flocks over the intervening miles? Or is he, despite Gottwald,[32] a Bedouin? In that case, in what sense does he "live" in Tekoa? There are other sycamores in Palestine, but these lie far to the north. To the north. . . .

Tosef. Shev. 7:11 (Pes. 53a) says, "Wherever sycamores do not grow is upper Galilee; wherever sycamores do grow is lower Galilee." Judean Amos might have gotten his figs from there, but the idea is farfetched. It

---

[30]Morris Jastrow, *Dictionary of Biblical and Targumic Aramaic* (New York: Pardes, 1950) 1:175. According to Wright, "Amos and the Sycamore," 362, Aquila uses ἐρευνάω, "to search, examine." This is interesting because Aquila is known for his excessive literalness. For other uses consult Joseph Reider, *Index to Aquila* (Leiden: E. J. Brill, 1966) 96. See also Joseph Arieti, "The Vocabulary of Septuagint Amos," JBL 93 (1974): 338-47.

[31]Thus G. A. Smith, *Amos, Hosea, and Micah,* 2nd ed. (New York: Harper, 1928) 77-78, refuting Oort.

[32]Norman K. Gottwald, "Sociological Method in the Study of Ancient Israel," in *Encounters with the Text,* ed. Martin Buss (Philadelphia: Fortress, 1979) 67-81, esp. 77.

makes more sense to suppose that Amos was a Northern Kingdom functionary, one of whose jobs was the oversight of sycamore trees held by the crown. If he had a position in the Northern government, his public appearance at Bethel, his apparent command of an audience, and his relatively lenient treatment at the hands of Amaziah are all readily explicable.

Let us summarize. Traditional scholarship bequeathed to us an Amos who was an uneducated migratory laborer supporting himself around Judean Tekoa but taking frequent trips to Ein Gedi as well as to the north—despite the recent civil war and the ill will in its aftermath—who became so well acquainted with Samarian social abuses that he could call his hosts to task for it, and who had the charisma to command their attention despite a public "ministry" of uncommon brevity. Is not such a reconstruction needlessly complicated? If there is any "hacking" to be done here, let's use Ockham's Razor to do it.

If Amos is a Northern civil servant, the need for the involved picture sketched above disappears. Amos's position in society gives him both status and familiarity with his country's practices and problems. Is Amos also a prophet? Initially, no. He will have been considered one, however, perhaps within his own lifetime. After all, he said, "I will rise against the house of Jeroboam with the sword" (7:9), at least three years before that house fell. After 723 there would be no longer any question.

Judeans would have welcomed Amos's views, and his person, long before his words proved prophetic. Amos himself, however, was probably not too concerned with how future generations would remember him. He was alarmed by his country's moral decay, enough to cry out against it at considerable risk to himself. "A shrewd person would remain silent in such an evil time" (my rendering of Amos 5:13). What did he see that caused him to forego a comfortable position in Israel in the (futile) attempt to warn his compatriots of their impending doom? The next chapter addresses this question.

5

Sociology of Samaria

Cry, the beloved country. —Alan Paton

Samuel was right, empire has its price.[1] The prosperity of an empire is never evenly divided; even before Israel embarked on its imperialistic campaigns the shift to a monarchy had already begun the process of increasing the economic disparities between classes. When Solomon died, the community (קָהָל) sought relief from excessive taxation by petitioning his son, Rehoboam. His famous answer, "My little finger is thicker than my father's loins" (1 Kgs 12:10), helped precipitate the secession of the northern tribes. But the new government that arose (finally) in Samaria was no more democratic than the old one had been.[2]

The institution of the monarchy and subsequent Israelite expansion eroded and then destroyed the older system by which peasant freeholders worked their ancestral lands. Robert Coote gives a positively blistering account of the evolution of Israel's land-tenure system from patriarchal to prebendary.[3] By Amos's time the expropriation of the peasantry had been

---

[1]The prophet's warnings (1 Sam 8:11-14) went unheeded.

[2]Roland de Vaux, *Ancient Israel. Its Life and Institutions* (New York: McGraw-Hill, 1961) 72ff., remarks on the disparity of wealth indicated by the Tirzah excavations. Tirzah, of course, was Omri's first capital. Samaria was much grander.

[3]Robert Coote, *Amos among the Prophets* (Philadelphia: Fortress, 1981) 24-32, acknowledges his debt to Wolf and Gottwald.

in process for 250 years--and not just of the peasantry, if the example of Naboth's vineyard can be taken as symptomatic.[4]

Recurring drought and famine, to which Amos alludes, would probably also affect society from the bottom up. We do not need to posit, as W. Robertson Smith does,[5] that it was largely the exigencies of war that depressed the lower classes. War itself does not produce natural disasters, but it does harvest a bumper crop of widows and orphans, easy prey for rapacious elements among the wealthier clans.[6]

Moreover, upper-class Samarians had reason to believe that they were different, better and better protected by a stronger god than those of their neighbors. Whatever happened at the "Red Sea" must have been spectacular, and only as far back in their history as Columbus is in ours. After the Exodus they came into a goodly land, the best in Palestine, and dispossessed the previous inhabitants, as Amos reminds them in his chapter 2.

When Israel itself split, the North emerged as the stronger of the two successor kingdoms and made alliances that helped it to survive foreign incursions. True, good relations with Phoenicia must have ruptured with the murder of Jezebel, but Jehu's usurping dynasty was now in its fourth generation and had given the kingdom a stability it had not previously enjoyed. Given a theology that saw success as a sign of divine favor,[7] smug Samarians had good reason to be self-satisfied.

In the midst of this "era of good feelings," Amos arose and argued that Israelite society was rotten at its core. As we shall shortly see, a closer look at his excoriation indicates that he knew well the situations he con-

---

[4]Recall that Israel's "system" might have been the product of a recent revolution from Amarna-age feudalism. More than twenty years ago Cyrus Gordon used to justify Jezebel on the grounds that she, a Phoenician, would not have understood how a subject could honorably refuse his king's request.

[5]W. Robertson Smith, *The Prophets of Israel and Their Place in History* (New York: D. Appleton, 1892) 95.

[6]It is almost a given that Israel at this time was experiencing a widening of the gulf between its classes. This idea is especially attractive, e.g., to Dijkema, who sees an almost Marxian progression taking place. I wonder, though, whether it would not be more appropriate to speak of clans than classes. Benjamin Mazar, "Tobiads," EJ 15:1,178-80, dates the rise of that clan in transjordan to the reign of Jeroboam II.

[7]Arvid S. Kapelrud, "New Ideas in Amos," VTSup 15 (1965): 202. This is Deuteronomic theology, appropriate in the Northern Kingdom, and supports the reading of Calah/Calneh in 6:2. Note the comparison between Egypt and Assyria in Ezekiel 31.

demned. His depth of knowledge—already remarked on—itself speaks to his having been a full-time member of that society. The terms he uses (see below) to identify the various groups of exploited persons have almost technical extensions relating to the ways in which each group was defrauded of rights or property.

As a member of the "haves," Amos had both knowledge of how the other half lives and sufficient status to make a public denunciation of the conditions that submerged them. Before launching this attack (and here we assume the order we have in Amos is the original order of his remarks), however, he engages in a series of oracles against foreign nations to which some attention should be paid.

This section in Amos (1:3–2:5) is often treated apart from the rest of the book. Indeed, James Barton has recently devoted a fine monograph to it,[8] in which much of the space is taken up with questions of "authenticity": Did Amos say all these things, or are some of them secondary? Adherents to both positions abound.[9] Both sides try to explain the present order of the oracles,[10] so that here it is especially difficult to say anything new and different, even if one feels the need. In fact, I would contend that a correct appreciation of these oracles was already produced by G. Johannes Botterweck's observation[11] that allows us to see how unified (and therefore authentic) the oracles are.

In Botterweck's view the whole passage works as a series of concentric rings of relationship. In the first and most-distant circle are Aram, Gaza (the Philistines), and Tyre (the Phoenicians), three of Israel's long-standing foreign rivals. In the second circle, closer to Israel, stand Edom, Ammon, and Moab, all related to the Israelites by blood, even if two are bastard

---

[8]James Barton, *Amos's Oracles against the Nations* (London: Cambridge University Press, 1980); see his bibliography. Probably no other part of Amos has drawn so much attention.

[9]This subject is discussed in the next chapter. My position is that all the oracles are probably genuine.

[10]Aage Bentzen theorizes they were modeled after the Egyptian Execration texts; Yehezkel Kaufmann proposes an alternating scheme—enemy of Israel, enemy of Judah, etc. This proposal assumes Israel and Judah are in most senses one unit, which we have seen is not the case. Shalom Paul attempts to tie all the oracles together literarily in "Amos 1:3–2:3. A Concatenous Literary Pattern," JBL 90 (1971): 397-403, and again in the Cazelles Festschrift— see n. 12.

[11]G. Johannes Botterweck, "Zur Authentizität des Buches Amos 2:6-8," ZAW 70 (1958): 176-89.

kin. The third and nearest circle is occupied by the estranged sister kingdom, Judah, alone.

We need some understanding of the oracles because any interpretation
of the Book of Amos partly depends upon how much of it originated with
the "Amos" we have identified and, consequently, what his viewpoint was.
For example, what happens if we exclude the oracle against Judah, as some
have proposed?[12] This is an attractive suggestion. It reduces the number of
oracles to seven (on Amos's use of sevens, see below), but implies that
Amos has no complaints about things in Judah. We have seen (above) that
the Judeans, too, would have had problems for prophets to address. Par-
enthetically, if the Judah oracle is an addition, then the original Amos is
all the more likely to have been a Northerner.

For all that, I think the Judah oracle is genuine, that all the oracles are.
Claims against them based upon variations in style, word choice (for instance, הִצַּתִּי in 1:14, addressed in chapter 7, below), or the lack of open-
ing/closing formulae only help to prove how authentic these pieces are.
Certainly, anyone who wished to insert an oracle into an Amos-text that
lay at hand would be careful to imitate the style. Amos himself, as we have
seen, was not a prophet and so might be less careful. He knew somewhat
of the prophetic and other speech forms,[13] but he was driven by a passion
that probably precluded punctiliousness. There is order here, but it is not
the order of the professional prophet and speechifier. We will have more
to say on this in the next chapter.

The number of oracles—seven plus the one against Israel—and their
order do show a unity of purpose. Gordis remarks on the presence of sevens in Amos; indeed, they are more prevalent than Gordis's article shows.[14]

---

[12]Those denying its authenticity include Barton, Driver, Eissfeldt, Mays, and
Wolff. Interestingly, William Rainey Harper, *A Critical and Exegetical Commentary on Amos and Hosea,* ICC (Edinburgh: T. & T. Clark, 1905) 44-45, gives
equal space to both arguments. Paul reaffirms his position in "A Literary Reinvestigation of the Authenticity of the Oracles against the Nations of Amos," *De
la torah au Messie,* ed. Maurice Carrez, Joseph Dore, and Pierre Grelot (Paris:
Descleé, 1981) 189-204.

[13]See Claus Westermann, *Basic Forms of Prophetic Speech* (Philadelphia:
Westminster, 1967). Form criticism has its uses, but it invites the sin of overcor-
recting the texts it operates on. The best example of this is D. Mueller's correction
of the "mistakes" in Ps 119 (see below, ch. 6 n.18). I think these were deliberate
errors, choices of the Psalmist that reflect a piety that does not allow humans to
attempt perfection in the things they create lest God take offense.

[14]Robert Gordis, "The Heptad as an Element in Biblical and Rabbinic Style,"
JBL 62 (1943): 17-26.

Of course, if one excised any single oracle (say, the one against Judah) one would have the magic number, and this is one reason some critics feel the Judah oracle is suspect.

On the other hand, Amos might have foreseen, even planned on, taking his audience off guard when he made Judah the seventh object of God's wrath.[15] Regardless, it seems clear that the set was composed as we have it for the ultimate purpose or criticizing Israel, Amos's own country, at a length nearly equal to all the others combined (eighteen verses versus fourteen, counting 3:1-2 as part of the Israel oracle). This suggests that Israel is as sinful as all the rest combined, which, in turn, explains God's impending wrath (3:2).

What moves a man to denounce his own country? And what will that critic expect those denunciations to produce? In the twentieth century we have had ''prophets'' who crusade for the public good and ''children of prophets'' who minister to those in need. It is not too much to suggest that the same feelings of compassion for the exploited and outrage at injustice moved in the breast of one whose ancestors practically invented our notion of social justice. No doubt Amos harbored some hope that his words might help avert the danger he saw. I do not think he had much hope, but whether or no,[16] he spoke under a kind of desperate compulsion that we have come to equate with divine inspiration.

If Israel was not completely sinful,[17] its wealthier clans were. Whatever one decides about the formula ''three, yea four'' in the oracles against the other nations, in the Israel oracle three plus four equals seven—the number of completeness even when used in negative situations.[18]

---

[15]Shalom Paul says Amos planned Judah to be seventh so the Israelites would be shocked by what follows. Erling Hammerschaimb, *The Book of Amos. A Commentary,* trans. John Sturdy (Oxford: Blackwell; New York: Schocken, 1970) 43, thinks, rather, that Amos's audience would know their turn was next.

[16]Thomas Overholt, ''Commanding the Prophets. Amos and the Problem of Prophetic Authority,'' CBQ 41 (1979): 517-32. Amos's expectations are not irrelevant and I address them later.

[17]As with many another issue, there is scholarly division regarding the extent of Israel's sinfulness and, consequently, who will be spared. The text of Amos— if all of it is from the same pen—is ambiguous enough to support many positions.

[18]Writers on this subject include Davis, Paul, Roth, Soper (see bibliography for titles). Meier Weiss's ''The Pattern of Numerical Sequence in Amos 1–2,'' JBL 86 (1967): 416-23, is the most luminous exposition. Hans Walter Wolff, *Joel and Amos,* Hermeneia (Philadelphia: Fortress, 1977) 115, admits that Amos's use of x, x + 1 is unlike Wisdom usage. See n.25, below.

Here is Amos's indictment:

1. selling צַדִּקִים ("innocent")[19] for money (2:6b)
2. (selling) אֶבְיוֹנִים ("defaulters") for (want of) (the price of) a pair of sandals or of a sandal strap (2:6bB)[20]
3. either (a) trampling the heads of דַּלִּים ("poor," but see below) into the ground or (b) hungering after the dust on the heads of דַּל, or (c) bruising the heads of דַּלִּים[21]
4. perverting the normal behavior of עֲנָוִים ("tenant farmers") (2:7aA)
5. violating sexual norms with (a) indentured servants, (b) one's own daughter-in-law, or (c) sacred prostitutes (2:7b)[22] (Hos 4:14)
6. distraining garments (see below, page 62) taken in pledge (8a)
7. drinking wine collected as fines or taxes (2:8b)[23]

It is difficult to navigate the shoals of alternatives, especially in numbers three and five, but it is necessary to make an attempt. Hans Walter Wolff makes a good case against reading 2:7b as a condemnation of sacred prostitution, and it would seem most scholars agree with him.[24] On the other

---

[19]Prof. K. R. Nilsson acquainted me with the Italian expression *tradittore traduttore*— "translators are traitors." Since these groups should be identified by the sorts of abuse to which each is particularly vulnerable, we should refrain from translating prematurely. In Spiegel's highly entertaining "Amos *v* Amaziah" (in *The Jewish Expression,* 38-65 [New York: Bantam, 1970]), he refers (42) to the victims of injustice as the "needy and poor." It is unfortunate that a speech about biblical conceptions of law and justice should be so casual with what are virtually technical terms from the field of sociology.

[20]Cf. ANET 441, the Wisdom of Ipu-wer. The metaphor is clear enough, even if the mechanism is not.

[21]All three possibilities have been suggested (a) by RSV, followed by NEB and NJPST/1985; (b) by AV, followed by JPS/1917; (c) by JB/1966. Translators seek assistance from other texts, e.g., NJPST/1985's use of Job 24:4, without also trying to determine what real-life situation is being addressed. Philology is not enough.

[22]Cf. Codex Hammurabi 119 and Hittite law 194 in ANET, 171 and 196 respectively. Lev 20:11 prohibits the practice, but this implies familiarity with it. Theodor Gaster, *Thespis* (New York: Harper, 1961) 42, notes that compulsory prostitution existed in India into the twentieth century.

[23]The prominence of wine on the Samarian Ostraca makes Hans Barstad's suggestion that we read here "rates" (= taxes) a good one: *The Religious Polemics of Amos* (Leiden: E. J. Brill, 1984) 15 n.19.

[24]Wolff, *Joel and Amos,* 167, depends on Lev 18:15 to suppose Amos refers to forbidden intercourse with one's daughter-in-law. Martinus Beek, "The Religious Background of Amos 2:6-8," OTS 5 (1948): 132-41, agrees.

hand, it is tempting to read נַעֲרָה as "hierodule" and the series as composed of four sins against fellow Israelites and three against God.[25] "For three and for four. . . . "

These explanations all smack a bit of midrash, but we need to try to produce a coherent picture of those conditions in the Northern Kingdom that Amos knew and opposed. Appreciation of Amos and his place in Northern Kingdom society depends in part on whether his criticism is general or a bill of particulars that an insider would have precise knowledge of and an outsider would not.

We know that Hebrew prophets, professional or part-time, fought an uphill battle to convince Israel that God and no other god was responsible for their well-being (see Josh 24). If we add to this the recollection that Samaria was the spiritual capital of the Canaanite elements in Israelite society[26] and that well-to-do Samarians would have the most reason to reject the prophetic call for exclusive Yahwism, we will conclude that Amos's remarks aim not only at lip-service Yahwists, but also at Samarian practices deriving from non-Israelite sources such as worship of astral deities and religious or casual copulation with slaves.[27]

Some of the people involved in these crimes are the same "cows of Bashan" whom Amos castigates elsewhere, for instance 4:1ff. and 6:1ff. The "cows of Bashan" (4:1) have been identified as adherents of a "dragon cult," but A. J. Williams's guess, that it is rather a fertility cult imported from Gilead, makes more sense.[28] Does not Hosea also criticize them (Hos

---

[25]The use of sequence numbers is well known and widespread in the Bible (see GKC 134s) and in the ancient Near East, but 3...4 may have special significance in Israel with its three patriarchs and four matriarchs. Georges Farr, "The Language of Amos," VT 16 (1966): 319, concurs— though not for the same reason. See also Wolfgang M. W. Roth, "The Numerical Sequence x/x + 1 in the Old Testament," VT 12 (1962): 300-11.

[26]Herbert Donner in John Hayes and Maxwell Miller, eds., *Israelite and Judean History* (Philadelphia: Westminster, 1977) 403, but it is Alt's idea, e.g., in "Monarchy," *Essays on O.T. History and Religion* (Garden City NY: Doubleday, 1968) 322.

[27]Jewish tradition has had little trouble co-opting such foreign or pre-Israelite practices as prayers to the New Moon. It is not so much the practices themselves that are objected to; rather, it is that this or that ceremony recognizes as legitimate an object of worship that is not God.

[28]A. J. Williams, "Further Suggestions about Amos 4:1-3," VT 29 (1979): 206-11. Cf. the women of Peor in Numbers 25. If this cult is Gileadite, it might be connected with the Tobiads.

12:12a[11a])? Sexual excesses would be typical of the מַרְזֵחַ, an institution
known to Amos (see commentary on 6:7 below), but until very recently
not known to biblical scholarship. Before discussing this crucial social institution, however, we will try more explicitly to define those whom the
wealthy dispossessed, usually lumped together as the "poor and needy."

In 1892, Alfred Rahlf's 'ānī und 'ānāw in den Psalmen[29] was the first
serious attempt to classify sections of the Israelite population below the ar-
istocracy. The assumption that the relevant texts were mostly late made
such study attractive to commentators who may have had one eye on the
"meek" of the New Testament period.[30] But Rahlf's work was effectively
refuted by Birkeland and Mowinckel[31] and is now largely neglected except
by those, such as Dijkema, whose ideological biases make them a priori
receptive to it.[32] The need to identify the groups remains.

Curiously, עָנִי and עָנָו are rare in Amos; he evidently prefers the terms
דַּל and אֶבְיוֹן.[33] Why? Most commentators seem content to identify either
pair as a sort of merism, like our "poor and needy," and see no need to

---

[29](Göttingen: Vandenhoeck und Rupprecht, 1892). Preliminarily regarding
עָנִי and אֶבְיוֹן, see Ernst Bammel, "The Poor in the Old Testament," §B. in the
article (885-915) on πτωχός, πτωχεία, πτωχεύς in vol. 6 of *Theological
Dictionary of the New Testament,* ed. Gerhard Friedrich, trans. Geoffrey W.
Bromiley (Grand Rapids MI: Eerdmans, 1968) 888-94.

[30]Beek, "Background," 140, and "New Ideas," 205, see these "poor and
needy" as the "just" par excellence. Are they backreading from the Sermon on
the Mount? Jesus said that one cannot serve both God and mammon, but does this
imply that impecunious people are automatically pious? For a discussion of the
Ebionites, see below. Ernst Bammel, at the end of a long article on πτωχός κτλ.
("poor"), concludes that "Ascetic tendencies in the early church led to opposition to property, . . . [and ultimately] almost completely obscured the legacy of
the OT and later Jewish view of the poor" (TDNT 6:915).

[31]Harris Birkeland, *Das Feinde des Individuums in der Israelitischen Psal-
menliteratur* (Oslo: Dybwad, 1933); Sigmund Mowinckel, *Psalmenstudien,* 1.
Awän und die individuellen Klagepsalmen, Skrifter utgitt av Det Norske Viden-
skaps-Akademi i Oslo (Kristiania [Oslo], 1921), and *The Psalms in Israel's Worship,* 2 vols., trans. D. R. ApThomas (Oxford: Basil Blackwell, 1962) 2:251.

[32]F. Dijkema, "Le Fond des Propheties d'Amos," OTS 2 (1943): 18-34, refers to Amos's period as the "second or 'commercial' phase of capitalism." Ideological offhandedness does not do justice to the text of Amos nor to the society
described in it. See also P. A. Munch, "Einige Bemerkungen zu den עֲנָוִים und
den רְשָׁעִים in den Psalmen," MO 30 (1936): 13-14.

[33]Again, if related words really were synonymous, it would be difficult to account for the word preferences of various texts. More on this below.

attempt a more exact identification of each member. Lately, however, thanks to Norman K. Gottwald and Edward R. Wolf, we have come to see biblical Israel as a society composed of various intersecting human groups, not just two-dimensional stage props for the mighty dramas of the acts of God. Coote[34] directs our attention to the existence of the lower socioeconomic strata and Amos's concern for them. If Amos prefers certain terms, they likely have specific denotations, not just connotations.

I propose that each term has a separate extension, that is to say a different meaning. Since we have already identified four terms in the same semantic field ("impecunious") without going beyond Amos and Psalms, it is reasonable to suppose that Amos's familiarity with the social shadings of Israel mark him as more than just a person sensitive to the misfortunes of others. Must he not have been a longtime member of and participant in that society he so accurately portrayed? We shall see.

The terms אֶבְיוֹן and דַּל are called "Wisdom terms" because more than fifty per cent of their occurrences are in the so-called Wisdom books—Job, Proverbs, and Psalms. Wolff[35] naturally sees this datum as support for his theory that Amos somehow derives from an ancient Near Eastern "wisdom tradition" in which Israel shared. But simply counting gross occurrences is not enough.

As table 3 shows, Psalms "prefers" אֶבְיוֹן by a count of twenty-three to five; Proverbs uses דַּל/דַּלִּים fourteen times and אֶבְיוֹן/ים only four times.

By itself this imbalance implies that these two terms are not synonyms, even more so if one accepts Goodman's definition, namely,

> two terms are synonymous if and only if . . . each compound term constructed by combining certain words with either of the terms in question applies to exactly the same objects as the compound term constructed by combining the same words in the same way with the other.[36]

---

[34]Coote, *Amos,* 36, extensively quotes Wolf, *Peasants* (Englewood Cliffs NJ: Prentice-Hall, 1966) and several of Gottwald's (137) works to this effect.

[35]Hans Walter Wolff, *Amos the Prophet,* trans. Foster McCurley (Philadelphia: Fortress, 1973) 166 n.277.

[36]N. Goodman, "On Some Differences about Meaning," in *Philosophy and Analysis,* ed. J. Macdonald (New York: Philosophical Library, 1954) 63-69. Robert Alter, *The Art of Biblical Poetry* (New York: Basic Books, 1985) 11, observes that "six" is not synonymous with "half a dozen" and if number designations are not synonymous, nothing is.

Table 3. Occurrences of Words Denoting "impecunious" in Psalms and Proverbs

LOC CIT	דַּל	אֶבְיוֹן	אַלְמָנָה	יָתוֹם
Psalms		9:19		
				10:14,18
		12:6		
		35:10		
		37:14		
		40:18(70:6)		
	41:2			
		49:3		
			68:6	68:6
		69:34		
	72:13	72:4,12,13		
		74:21		
	82:3,4	82:4		82:3
		86:1		
			94:6	94:6
		107:41		
		109:16,22,31	109:9	109:9,12
		112:9		
	113:7	113:7		
		132:15		
		140:13		
			146:9	146:9
Proverbs	10:15			
	14:31	14:31		
			15:25	
	19:4,17			
	21:13			
	22:9,16,22			
				23:10
	28:3,8,11,15			
	29:7,14			
		30:14		
		31:9		
		31:20		

To put it in the blunter manner favored by Cassuto, "as a rule, synonyms are not quite identical in meaning."[37] If this is so, then we are all the more obliged to determine the differences between closely related words whether

---

[37]Umberto Cassuto, *The Documentary Hypothesis and the Composition of the Pentateuch* (Jerusalem: Magnes, 1961) 18. But now see Isaac Kikawada, *Before Abraham Was* (Nashville: Abingdon, 1987), a reading of Gen 1–11 as a unit, not a documentary patchwork.

they occur in prose or, as here, in poetry.[38]

Unfortunately, the parallel construction of so much Wisdom literature gives rise to the easy assumption that words used in parallel are equivalent, even identical: proponents of this view could cite the uses of דַּל and אֶבְיוֹן in Psalms 72 and 82. Insisting that three cases of parallelism means that two terms are synonymous is a bit like defenders of Aristotle's notions of gravity continuing to defend him because, in fact, the heavier of the two balls Galileo dropped from the tower at Pisa did hit the ground a bit before the lighter one. How do we explain Psalms' marked preference for one of two words if they mean the same thing? As Kugel advises us, poetic parallels are simply not conclusive evidence of synonymity.[39]

If more proof were needed, I should point out that Deuteronomy uses אֶבְיוֹנִים seven times and does not use דַּלִּים even once. Considering the supposed influence of Deuteronomy on Amos (we will argue that the converse if the case),[40] it is worth investigating the treatment of אֶבְיוֹנִים in Deuteronomy 15, a chapter that contains almost all of the book's use of the term.

Here it is apparent that אֶבְיוֹנִים are marginal agriculturalists, already debtors, who face ruin if they cannot obtain additional loans even at outrageous rates of interest. When Sabbatical approaches, credit of any sort dries up—a situation that would only be remedied by the legal fiction of *prozbul* (literally "corridor," understood in rabbinic literature as a way around the letter of the law requiring remission of debts) invented by Hillel the Elder just before Jesus' time. Since one cannot plant during Sabbatical, the impecunious might very well be forced to sell themselves or their children into some form of indentured servitude. Indeed, Deuteronomy 15:12 continues with rules governing the treatment of Hebrews sold to other Hebrews.

---

[38]The line is hard to draw. See Alter, *Art*, 5-6. Also still helpful is George Buchanan Gray, *The Forms of Hebrew Poetry* (New York: KTAV, 1969/1915).

[39]James Kugel, *The Ideas of Biblical Poetry* (New Haven CT: Yale University Press, 1981) 302ff., though it is his recurring theme. See also Samuel Sandmel, "Parallelomania," JBL 81 (1962): 1-14.

[40]Fifty years ago, Hans Krause saw "Die Gerichtsprophet Amos, [als] ein Vorlaufer des Deuteronomisten," ZAW 50 (1932): 221-39. Duane Christensen, *Transformations of the War Oracle in Old Testament Prophecy* HDR 3 (Missoula MT: Scholars Press, 1975) 57-72, also thinks Deuteronomic thought has a northern origin. Ginsberg, *The Israelian Heritage of Judaism* (New York: Jewish Theological Seminary, 1982) 19-24, makes it even clearer that Amos and Deuteronomy live on a two-way street.

True, the term דַּל is used parallel with אֶבְיוֹן twice in Psalms and once in Proverbs (14:31), but their situations are hardly comparable. דַּלִּים are not rich—quite the opposite[41]—but Exodus 30:15 does not excuse them from the half-shekel tax. If the דַּל is leprous, he/she must still present one-third of the usual offering (Lev 14:21). As noted, Deuteronomy does not use the term, but it does contain various verses legislating protection for widows and orphans.

I suggest that דַּלִּים ("small freeholders") is a generic term for those persons without sufficient male (or tribal) protection or status to avoid exploitation by the more powerful. Such a group might also include sojourners (גֵּרִים, such as Abraham was in Egypt) and, to a lesser extent, Levites—the same subgroups Deuteronomy goes to some lengths to protect, for example, in 10:18; 24:17, 19-21; 26:12-13; 27:19. Of these verses, Deuteronomy 24:17 has special relevance here.

The parallel passage, Exodus 22:26, prohibits keeping one's neighbor's garment, taken in pledge, overnight, but Deuteronomy 24:17 specifies it as a widow's garment. Given the time-proximity between Amos and proto-Deuteronomy, it is possible Amos know Northern Kingdom "torah" and that it prohibited the very thing he was witnessing (2:8).

Both דַּלִּים and אֶבְיוֹנִים may be victims of injustice sponsored by or connived at by the state (see also Am 8:6), but the weight of our evidence suggests the two terms are not interchangeable. דַּלִּים seem particularly prone to fines in kind (5:11), implying they possess something of value. This indicates that the best translation of 2:7a (above) is "hungering after the dust on the heads of small freeholders," a hyperbole for the last little bit of "land" they possess and, by the way, a much more serious charge than the other two readings can sustain.[42] (It is worth investigating the similarity between Hebrew דַּל and Hindi *dalita*.)

At this point Coote offers a key insight. Why were big estate owners so anxious to acquire the lands of others? Why not settle for permanent

---

[41]See Exod 30:5; Ruth 3:10; also Lev 19:15. If the Phoenician cognate sheds any light (CIS 165.15, cited by Z. S. Harris, *Phoenician Grammar* [Philadelphia: Jewish Publication Society, 1936] 95), they are not completely poverty-stricken.

[42]The difficulty inheres in determining the root. Is it שָׁאַף or שׁוּף? Albin van Hoonacker, "Notes d'exégèse sur quelques passages difficiles d'Amos," RB 14 (1905): 163-87, esp. 163-64, follows Vulgate's *conterunt* and reads "bruise." The א could be a medial *mater lectionis*: see Ernst Würthwein, *The Text of the Old Testament*, trans. Peter R. Ackroyd (London: Blackwell, 1962) 74. We ought not let the philological forest obscure the trees. As Alter, *Art,* 140, says, "Prophetic poetry . . . is devised as a form of direct address to a historically real audience."

serfdom of the lower classes (represented by what happens to the אֶבְיוֹנִים, below)? Coote's answer[43] is that the major landlords coveted additional land because they were engaged in the export of wine and olive oil to support their newly acquired taste for foreign luxury items such as the ivories found at Samaria.[44]

Peasant farms were usually devoted to the kind of mixed agriculture that could directly support only the people living on them. This would be of little use to an economy increasingly based on import and export. Hence, the rich attempted to "add field to field" (Is 5:8ff., a passage reminiscent of Amos) and to break the peasants' hold on the land. Those אֶבְיוֹנִים who were already debtors were in constant danger of being dispossessed for further debt, even to so small a value as "a sandal strap." (This metonymy is strikingly like our metaphor, "living on a shoestring." One wonders what those early Jewish-Christians who called themselves Ebionites meant by the term and why they chose it rather than one of the other, related words.)

Selling צַדִּיקִים for money (2:6b) means either employing bribery to obtain favorable judgments against innocent people of modest means or, literally, as Lang thinks, selling people into slavery for debt.[45] If Amos refers to Hebrews being sold, they were probably small freeholders who had taken out loans using their land—or their children—as collateral and were guilty only of a failure to make stipulated repayments.

Seen in this context, the charge of sexual misconduct in 2:7b probably refers to forced intercourse with indentured servants, people whose economic position had put them at the mercy of their new masters. The legislation in Exodus 21:7-11 tries to preclude abuses of the indenture, but prohibition presupposes previous practice: the laws are doubtless a reaction to an existing situation, not an anticipation of it. My choice of interpretation, of course, does not rule out the other possibilities. Amos may intend the ambiguity we feel here.

What class or kind of people does Amos identify as עֲנָוִים (2:7) and עַנְוֵי־אָרֶץ (8:4)? They are peasants, probably tenant farmers who are cheated by the merchant class. That they are tenant farmers, not freeholders, cannot be demonstrated from this text, but may be inferred from context. I

---

[43]Coote, *Amos,* 33-34.

[44]Selections may be found in ANET, DOTT, and Yohanan Aharoni, *The Land of the Bible* (Philadelphia: Westminster, 1967) 315-27. The latter is the most complete.

[45]Bernhard Lang, "Sklaven und Unfreie im Buch Amos (2:6–8:6)," VT 31 (1981): 482-88.

think Peter Andreas Munch[46] is right when he reads 2:7 as indicating that the "customary use of the peasants/עֲנָוִים" was to turn over the land they worked to their children even though they did not own it—the same situation that is at the root of the Israeli-Palestinian problem today. For all the reasons stated above, this was becoming less and less possible in Amos's time.

Amos seems aware of these dislocations in two other places. The first is in 7:1ff. where the locusts attack after the king (or landlord) gets his share but before the sharecropper harvests his. The second is Amos's warning (5:11), "you have planted pleasant vineyards, but you shall not drink their wine." The use of figurative language ought not confuse us: this is more than metaphor.

To summarize, the picture one gets is of rapacious upper classes doing any manner of fraud in order to possess themselves of the farms of freeholders. These lands they plant in wine grapes in order to partake of the profits from the export trade. But it takes three years for vines to produce any wine and seven or eight for commercially valuable quantities.[47] In Amos's estimation, Israel won't last that much longer.

We do not know how Amos himself felt about wine. He complains (2:12) that his countrymen pressed wine on Nazirites, and while one could see this simply as symbolic of a sybaritic society, I think there is a specific locus to which Amos refers. Hosea, Amos's younger contemporary, indicates that intoxication and sexual excesses were usual practices of deviant Israelites occupying high government positions.[48] We will now see under what circumstances these deviations took place, namely, in the מַרְזֵחַ.

Until recently, very little was known about the מַרְזֵחַ, since Scripture includes the term only in Amos 6:7 and Jeremiah 16:5. The word has a root yielding either "revelry" (Amos) or "mourning cry" (Jeremiah). In fact, these two verses indicate two of its major functions as we know them from

---

[46]Peter Andreas Munch, "Einige Bemerkungen zu den עֲנָוִים und den רְשָׁעִים in den Psalmen," MO 30 (1936): 13-14.

[47]Prof. Craig Houston, Dickinson College Economics Department, private communication. (Houston operates his own vineyard.) Arcadius Kahan's evaluation of the industry in biblical Israel indicates an even longer waiting period was necessary then: "Economic History," EncJud 16:1,268. Nachum Gross, *Economic History of the Jews* (Jerusalem: Keter, 1975) adds, "But the ultimate returns were quite rewarding in produce yielded from small plots of land."

[48]Hosea passim. Some of Hosea's language is metaphorical, but some is not, e.g., 4:11; 7:5.

evidence that stretches from Ugarit to Palmyra[49] and from the fourteenth century B.C.E. to the third C.E. Jonas Greenfield tells us that

> the description [in Amos] matches the classical *thiasos,* especially the *triclinium,* and lists the elements that are also known from Palmyra almost a thousand years later.[50]

In Israel as elsewhere, the מַרְזֵחַ was a socioreligious group composed of and catering to the affluent. The two scriptural verses bracket its function as a combination country club and burial society.[51] The members might have a house (6:9; see also RS 15.88)[52] where they recline on ivory couches (6:4), make music "like David" (6:5),[53] drink wine from (silver) bowls of the sort associated with temple offerings (Num 7; Hosea hints that these were supplied by priest-members), and anoint themselves with the finest oil (6:6). Wine and oil, of course, are just the two commodities we find docketed in the famous Samaria Ostraca, attributed to the reign of Jeroboam II, which are presumably the product of crown lands, taxes, or fines. If the last, we should recall Amos's complaint in 2:8 that "they" drink wine collected as fines—at the urging of their wives, perhaps (4:1).

We already saw that Amos castigates the "cows of Bashan." Is it the Bull of Bashan they worship (see above)? And if this imported Gileadite religion includes fertility rites, then another of Amos's earlier criticisms (2:7) would apply: "Father and son go into the same girl, and thereby profane my holy name." Surely, this is a reference to sacred prostitution. Seen in this light, the much-discussed 6:13 could have a third *entendre.* קַרְנַיִם

---

[49]Jonas Greenfield, "The MARZEAH as a Social Institution," in *Wirtschaft und Gesellschaft in alten Vorderasien,* ed. Joseph Harmatta (Budapest: Akademiai Kiodo, 1974-1976) 451-55. He notes it in KAI nos. 60 and 69.

[50]Ibid., 453. Coote, *Amos,* 38, offers "fellowship of those who keel over" as a rough translation.

[51]In ch. 6 we discuss foreign words in Amos, but we should point out here that G. R. Driver sees the Samarian term *śk* glossed over in 6:10's hapax legomenon מְסָרְפוֹ: "A Hebrew Burial Custom," ZAW 66 (1954): 314-15. This observation, made years before we knew about the *marzeah,* would fit in very well with its activities.

[52]Greenfield, "MARZEAH," 452. (Other recent studies are cited by the editor in Wolff, *Joel and Amos,* 277 n.48.

[53]Wellhausen's tendentious emendation of כְּדָוִיד ("like David") to כַּד וְיָד ("clapping potsherds together") is an example of what happens when we understand biblical texts according to a preordained schema.

might refer to bulls' horns that male members of the מַרְזֵחַ cult don for ritual, sexual purposes.[54] (Can we assign the admittedly murky 6:10 to this locus?)

Even if this last conjecture is not correct, Amos 6:1-10 (with the possible exception of verse 8, which we will discuss in chapter 7) gives a picture of overindulgence at once dramatic and clear. It is so clear that if the house in 6:9 is a מַרְזֵחַ ''clubhouse,'' we may wish to consider transposing 5:3 here, obtaining ''The city that sends out 1,000 shall get back 100, if 100 then ten, and if ten people are left in a house, they shall die.'' Things usually associated with life are now associated with death. As 1:2 implies,[55] the world is turning upside down.

If I may suggest a rather free translation of Amos 6:4-7 it would be

> [4]who sleep on beds of ivory,
>   and stretch out on couches;
> who eat lambs from the flock,
>   and calves from the stall;
> [5]who compose for the lute, like David,
>   make instruments for song:
> [6]who drink wine from silver bowls,
>   and anoint themselves with virgin oil,
>   giving no thought to the rest of Joseph;
> [7]inevitably, they will lead the exiles,
>   and the sound of their singing cease.
>   (or: the prince of revels will putrefy).

To us, of course, the מַרְזֵחַ members' behavior is reprehensible, and we wonder that any Israelites could have so debauched themselves. Such a criticism would be anachronistic. As Barstad[56] correctly reminds us, the

---

[54]Given the prevalence of totemism in the ancient world, it would be strange if the Hebrews were at no time involved. And more than just ''involved,'' if Raphael Patai's theories of *The Hebrew Goddess* (New York: KTAV, 1967) are correct and Asherah was widely worshipped in Israel. Knowledge of these things might be lost now for, certainly, they would have been avoided if not suppressed during the later biblical and rabbinic periods.

[55]This ''motto,'' which so many commentators see as added (see ch. 6, below), serves a major thematic role in Amos: everything that used to be secure and trusted will now prove vain and false, and example of which is the ''Day of the Lord'' with no light in it. Prof. Nahum Sarna first drew this to my attention.

[56]Barstad, *Polemics,* 10.

question for our Hebrew forebears was whether God or various of the *ba'alim* were ultimately responsible for the land's fertility and thus were deserving objects of worship. According to Greenfield, the *thiasos* was "dedicated to a particular god"; this might have been God, but given the outstanding possibility that Samaria was a center of Canaanite worship, it is more likely that such *ba'alim* as Ashima of Hamath or the god of Dan, to note two whom Amos names,[57] would be venerated.

At this point it is interesting to focus on the peculiar omission of any criticism of the Golden Calf, the *ba'al* par excellence. Amos, like Elijah and Elisha, is anti-*ba'al* but not anti-calf.[58] Some have thought[59] that Amos was "tempering the wind to the shorn lamb"; in other words, that he omitted it because he was afraid of being too critical and thus losing his audience. Such caution would be quite out of character. Moreover, the argument is absurd. Amos had already said more than the land could bear (7:10) and followed it with the vehement attack on Amaziah.

Just here, I urge, is incontrovertible proof that Amos was a Northerner and that his book suffered little editing at the hands of later Judean editors. Our ancestors, the Judean historians who compiled the Bible, make it appear as though Jeroboam I, in his haste to wean people away from Jerusalem, arbitrarily invented the calf as a symbol; but we know this is not true—just as we know it was no coincidence that when Aaron threw the

---

[57]I was at Tel Dan in 1976 when the bilingual inscription "To the god who is at Dan" was found. Greenfield, "MARZEAH," 451, tells us that the *marzeah* is usually dedicated to a particular god. Amos 5:25-26 also provides possible candidates. Deut 4:19 is one passage that warns against astral deities. Amos 5:8-9 repeats the Yahwistic contention that it is God who makes the constellations rise and set. G. R. Driver, "Two Astronomical Passages in the Old Testament," JTS n.s. 4 (1953): 208-12. But see below, ch. 6, n.41.

[58]William Foxwell Albright, *Yahweh and the Gods of Canaan* (Garden City NY: Doubleday, 1969) 199-200, notices that the use of the calf or bull as a legitimate accessory to Israelite worship was in some dispute as early as the twelfth century. Given Solomon's use of twelve bulls to carry the "great sea" outside his temple, names like Egelyau on the Samaria Ostraca, and Amos's silence on the subject, I expect the bull to have had as extensive as use as Moses' serpent (see 2 Kgs 18:4).

[59]Overholt, "Commanding the Prophets," and Yehoshua Gitay, "A Study of Amos's Art of Speech. A Rhetorical Analysis of Amos 3:1-15," CBQ 42 (1980): 293-309.

Israelites' gold into the fire (Exod 32:24) what came out, to his feigned surprise, was a calf and not a kangaroo.[60]

The calf or bull as an object of veneration is known all over the ancient Near East from earliest times; it should be no surprise to see it incorporated in Israelite worship, especially among Northerners. In the next chapter I discuss questions of the text's unity and authenticity, but the reader must already realize that no Judean editor could have failed to put criticism of the "sin of Jeroboam ben Nebat which he made Israel to sin" (2 Kgs 13:2 passim) into the mouth of Amos after the fact. After 723, the opportunity to criticize the calf would have been golden: they would not have missed it.

We have noted the name *Egelyau* in the Ostraca; there are also many names with *ba'al* theophoric elements. Could all of them be native Canaanites? It is unlikely. King Saul's sons Meriba'al, Ishba'al, and Jonathan serve as a trenchant example of the kind of group interpenetration that went on in Israel from its inception.

The literary qualities of this section (6:1-10) are discussed in the next chapter, but I must mention the possible wordplay-cum-scriptural allusion between סְרֻחִים in verses 4 and 7 and שְׂרוֹךְ־נַעַל in the well-known story of Abraham's rescue of Lot (Gen 14:23). Abraham won't accept so much as a "sandal strap" (שְׂרוֹךְ־נַעַל in Gen 14:23) from Melchizedek. The affluent ("recliners"—סְרֻחִים), who foreclose on אֶבְיוֹנִים for debts as insignificant as the price of a sandal strap, will themselves be forcibly "foreclosed" as though they, too, counted for nothing to those more powerful than they. This is the more so if Amos 4:3 can be translated to mean each of the "cows of Bashan" is to be dragged out through a breach in the wall of her own house[61] and thrown on the dungheap.[62]

---

[60]See Cyrus H. Gordon, *Ugarit and Minoan Crete* (New York: Norton, 1966). Mary Renault's *The Bull from the Sea* (New York: Pantheon, 1962) is a compelling fictional reconstruction of the place of bulls in Cretan society. Both Apis and Hathor are bovine dieties in Egypt, and Taurus, the bull of heaven, is known thoughout the Semitic world including, perhaps, Amos 5:8-9. (See above, n.57.)

[61]There is something about city architecture implied in 4:3. Kathleen Kenyon, *Royal Cities of the Old Testament* (New York: Schocken, 1971) 82, tells us that ground-floor casemates contained functional rooms. Seconded by Philip J. King, *Amos, Hosea, Micah—An Archaeological Commentary* (Philadelphia: Westminster, 1988). But did people live in them? If so, Amos's prediction becomes a literal description.

[62]To be cast on the "dungheap" (4:3, following T. H. Robinson and Norman Snaith; NEB has "dunghill") is a translation that makes an interesting merism with

Are all these allusions really here? Barton observes, "Amos does emerge as an intellectual whose ability to use literary tricks is not surprising."[63] Just how clever Amos was is the subject of our next chapter, regarding the unity and authenticity of the text.

---

marzeah. Other suggestions include "Hermon" (JB, NJB), "palace" (AV), and NJPST's halfhearted "refuse heap" (as also Smith/Goodspeed AT). Also, Ben Zion Luria's "harem" meaning "Assyria" and David Noel Freedman's *Harmon,* a site near Riblah—see bibliography.

[63]Barton, *Amos's Oracles,* 37.

6

Unity and Authenticity

Rhetorical prose . . . is naturally best adapted to the two purposes of rhetoric, ornament and persuasion.   —Northrop Frye

Aside from people whose religious beliefs compel them to accept the Bible's books as if all were engraved in stone, no one believes the Scriptures we have now are much like those left by their authors.[1] But scholarly opinion is often dogmatic also, subject to its own times and tides. Right now, with regard to Amos, the tide of reductionist scholarship is still in. If we were to accept all the deletions scholars suggest, we would dismiss from a half to two-thirds of Amos as secondary.

Coote claims three "levels" of Amos editorial activity, Wolff wants six, and Susamu Jozaki eight.[2] It is almost as if scholars were trying to outbid each other, leading John Bright to ask whether we can really subdivide a text of only 146 verses with such accuracy.[3]

---

[1]Joseph Blenkinsopp, *A History of Prophecy in Israel* (Philadelphia: Westminster, 1983) 93, works back "through the editorial process to find the man." The process is taken for granted. See n.3 below.

[2]Robert Coote, *Amos among the Prophets* (Philadelphia: Fortress, 1981) 1ff.; Hans Walter Wolff, *Joel and Amos,* Hermeneia (Philadelphia: Fortress, 1977) 1ff.; Susamu Jozaki, "The Secondary Passages of the Book of Amos," *Kwansei Gakuin University Annual Studies* 4 (1956): 25-100.

[3]John Bright, review of Hans Walter Wolff's *Joel and Amos* (1st German ed., 1969), *Interpretation* 25 (1971): 355-56. Recall (above, p. 4) Spinoza's remark on Hosea.

Irwin's approach[4] reduces the Amos-text to a series of apothegms. Even so conservative a scholar as Yeḥezkel Kaufman is willing to concede Amos is a "composite of various collections."[5] But as early as 1915 one can detect the beginning of a sea change.

In that year Hermann Gunkel proposed that copyists had no artistic freedom to change what lay in front of them.[6] At what point did the books pass into their hands? With our love for categorizing texts, we speak of a "prophetic canon" as though the whole were analogous to the musical works of the Bach family. Of course we know the prophets' activities took place over a period of centuries during which each "book" was probably the private property of that prophet's followers. Whatever the case, we must not assume there was only one legitimate, authorized version of each prophet's work so that enterprising editors or sloppy scribes could decisively influence the contents of the books with no chance their changes would be discovered and objected to.[7] Yet this is just the kind of assumption made by scholars who characterize textual difficulties as due to deficient copying[8] or excessive piety.

Nor should we assume the "prophetic canon" grew like a snowball rolling downhill, with each successive prophet falling heir to the work and the thought of all the former. Each prophetic book must be judged against

---

[4]William A. Irwin, "The Thinking of Amos," AJSL 49 (1933): 102-14. At the other extreme is William A. Smalley, "Recursion Patterns and the Sectioning of Amos," BT 30 (1979): 118-27, who makes of Amos a seamless garment centered on 5:9. The problem with this approach is that it makes Amos's text completely artificial.

[5]Yehezkel Kaufmann, *The Religion of Israel* (Chicago: University of Chicago Press, 1960) 364.

[6]E.g., G. R. Driver's remark ("Two Astronomical Passages in the Old Testament," JTS n.s. 4 [1953]: 209) anent 5:8-9: "some copyist, who misunderstood the purport of the last two lines, put it after . . . whereas it ought to follow. . . . "

[7]Hermann Gunkel, "Die Propheten als Schriftsteller und Dichter," cited by J. Willis, "Redaction Criticism and Historical Reconstruction," in *Encounter with the Text,* ed. Martin Buss (Philadelphia: Fortress, 1979) 85. Ḥaim Tadmor seconds this—"editors did not impose their views on the material"—in Haim-Hillel Ben-Sasson, ed., *A History of the Jewish People* (London: Weidenfeld and Nicholson, 1969) 113.

[8]The Talmud gives evidence that, in Second Temple times, three copies of Scripture were kept on file, as it were, to use as guides for other manuscripts. Only Solomon Zeitlin's article in Schnayer Z. Leiman, ed., *The Canon and Masorah of the Hebrew Bible* (New York: Arno, 1974) disputes this.

its own historical background before any comparisons are made. This is especially true for Amos because of his relative chronological priority.[9]

The guiding assumptions of this section are (1) that there is nothing in the Book of Amos the original Amos could not have written;[10] and (2) that (with Freedman and Andersen) the editing of Amos, even more than the editing of Hosea, was concluded "in living memory of those concerned."[11]

This is not to say that nothing in Amos differs from what the prophet himself first uttered. However, our obligation is first to consider the text as we have it and then try to see how its present form might retain or reflect the prophet's own words and thoughts.

Certainly the major stumbling block to any assertion of "unity" in Amos is the consensus of claims made regarding the secondary quality of the latter part of chapter 9. Starting at various points between 9:8 and 9:11, scholars have all but unamimously concluded that the ending is tacked on, and not very well at that.

Wellhausen rages that the prophet could not, would not, suddenly reverse himself as Amos does: in the midst of "blood and iron" Amos introduces "roses and lavender." Here, the great documentarist tells us, we have "a later Jew who has appended this coda, and removed the genuine conclusion, because this sounded harshly in his ears."[12] Other scholars

---

[9]Certainly, Amos's influence on subsequent prophets, especially Isaiah, Jeremiah, and Joel can hardly be denied, but other connections should be made with caution.

[10]S. R. Driver, *The Books of Joel and Amos,* 2nd ed. (Cambridge: Cambridge University Press, 1915) 115-126.

[11]Francis I. Andersen and David Noel Freedman, *Hosea. A New Translation with Introduction and Commentary,* AB 24 (Garden City NY: Doubleday, 1980) 147.

[12]Julius Wellhausen, *Die kleinen Propheten übersetzt und erklärt* ([3]1898), 96, cited in Georg Fohrer's edition of Ernst Sellin's *Introduction to the Old Testament,* trans. D. E. Green (Nashville: Abingdon, 1968) 436. E.g., Robert Martin-Achard and S. Re'emi's assertion that after 587 B.C.E., "People then felt the need . . . to set a limit to a message that was above all negative by including a word of consolation" (*Amos and Lamentations: God's People in Crisis,* ITC [Grand Rapids MI: Eerdmans, 1984] 6). One can certainly imagine later Jews wanting to find consolation in Scripture, but suppressing Amos's original conclusion seems a curious way of going about it. Even the ending to Ecclesiastes is apparently an addition, not a substitution.

The section has its defenders: Weiser, Mays, and Hammerschaimb. The latter (*The Book of Amos* [Oxford: Blackwell, 1970] 139) sees the possibility for Judean survivors of the coming calamity.

reason that the "fallen tabernacle of David" in 9:11 must refer to the destroyed First Temple and hence to sometime after 586 B.C.E.[13] Morgenstern[14] confidently assigns verse 12's "remnant of Edom" to 485 B.C.E.

To borrow a phrase from Wellhausen himself, I have to ask whether the firemen are coming near the spot where the conflagration rages, namely, in Amos's own immediate historical situation and his considerable knowledge of it.

We know—as Amos surely did—that relations between the two kingdoms, Israel and Judah, were fragile. But each had expansionist ambitions that should have dictated that both keep their common border quiet. Nonetheless, first one and then the other disturbed the status quo. We saw (above) what gave rise to these events. The consequences, *pace* Herrmann, are just as clear to us. Why not to Amos, who was so much closer to them?

As I reconstruct it, the situation in Amos's time was as follows. The battle between Israel and Judah, leading to the capture of Amaziah, proved to be a blessing in disguise for Judah. Kings gives his successor, Uzziah, short shrift, but Chronicles reports a series of successes,[15] suggesting Judah made a rapid recovery. Growing power in Judah would be of concern to Israel. Amos's prophecy that the fallen tabernacle would be raised again means that Judah would soon outstrip Israel. Indeed, it is less a prophecy and more a description of current events.

Not that the Judeans had everything going their way. Second Chronicles 25:20ff. indicates the Edomites were carrying their war to Judah by Ahaz's time (735). Thus, Amos 9:13's "remnant of Edom" need not refer

---

[13]Despite the scholarly consensus, it is hard to imagine such a vague, elegiac reference to Solomon's temple here. If Isaiah could "predict" the coming of Cyrus by name (45:1), Amos could be more specific about future events, too, especially after the fact! H. Neil Richardson, "SKT (Amos 9:11) 'Booth' or 'Succoth'?" JBL 92 (1973): 375-81, suggests we read SKT as a place name. For my view, see below, n.41.

[14]Julian Morgenstern, "Jerusalem—485 B.C.E.," HUCA 27 (1956): 101-80; HUCA 28 (1957): 15-48; HUCA 31 (1960): 1-30. Brevard S. Childs takes just the opposite tack: "By the linking of exegesis directly to historical reconstruction the integrity of the biblical text and the theological enterprise is seriously jeopardized." *Introduction to the Old Testament as Scripture* (Philadelphia: Fortress, 1979) 408.

[15]Yohanan Aharoni and Michael Avi-Yonah, *Macmillan Bible Atlas,* 2nd ed. (New York: Macmillan, 1977) 90 (map 114) show the extent of Uzziah's conquests.

to postexilic events. There is no need to reach down in history to 586 B.C.E., much less to 485 B.C.E., to make sense of the latter part of chapter 9, or of any part of the text.

Since a condition amounting to civil war still obtained between the kingdoms, the announcement that the house of Jeroboam would "die by the sword" (7:9) is exactly what the priest Amaziah termed it—"treason." No other prophet, even if he predicts ruin for his country, suggests it will be eclipsed by its rival. Amos does. Better times are coming, but it is Judah that will have them.

Is there, then, no part of Amos that is not original, and how might we determine which parts are not? Even if 9:8ff. is original, a conservative stance might still exclude Amos 1:1, 2; 3:7, plus the oracles against Tyre, Edom, and Judah, and the so-called doxologies (4:13; 5:8; 9:5-6), and suggest that 7:10-17 is at least out of place. Scholars also argue about the five visions, their placement and authenticity:[16] it is assumed that the fourth and fifth, not in the "style" of Amos, are consequently not from his pen. My position here is even more conservative.

The refutation of the first contention, as I indicated in chapter 5 above, is that if "Deuteronomic redactors" had really wanted to convince the community that Amos had said these new things, they should have cast the additions in language as indistinguishable from Amos's own as possible. Amos's consistent use of many speech forms points, I think, to the authenticity of precisely those pieces that look most intrusive.

On the other hand, the Judah oracle does look as though it has been tampered with, eviscerated, or at least damped down to spare Southern sensibilities after the fall of the First Temple. That could account for its lack of a closing formula, too, but how then explain the same lack in the oracle against Tyre?

Amos 1:1 is certainly added, but now soon after the completion of Amos's "ministry" and by whom are questions not easily answered. Since the superscription gives us a date congruent with the content of Amos, that is, since its writer knows nothing of the Ephraim-Gilead split of 752 B.C.E. or the murder of Jeroboam's son that preceded it, the prophet could have written 1:1 himself, though it is unlikely he did.

---

[16]In 1929 Weiser logically deduced that Amos's visions must have preceded his public appearance and so divided the text into a "book of visions" and a "book of words," cited approvingly in John D. W. Watts, *Vision and Prophecy in Amos* (Grand Rapids MI: Eerdmans, 1958) 27, 50.

Amos 1:2 is problematic. On the one hand, it is very much in the style of the rest of Amos. That it is widely considered the book's "motto"[17] is testimony to its use of language and thought that is wholly consistent with what follows. On the other hand, the use of "Jerusalem" here is or might be a premature tipping of the prophet's hand. If he wants to surprise his Northern audience by putting the Judah oracle seventh and then following with the long oracle against Israel, why identify Jerusalem as God's dwelling place in advance? Again, this looks like a bit Amos could have added after his expulsion, but forcing answers to such questions is bootless. In the case of Amos, it is enough to suggest we stop insisting the book be written as nineteenth-century exegetes would have written it.[18]

In regard to the second of the above contentions, Lindblom expresses proper caution when he says, "It would be too much to expect the collector to have produced an entirely logical order."[19] For all that, the internal logic of Amos—its author probably his own "collector"—is greater than most moderns recognize. William A. Smalley makes of the entire book a single unit revolving around 5:9.[20] I fail to see such tight organization in a piece that was delivered in a fit of passion (no matter that its author had time to ponder and refine it later). We must remember that the whole book could be spoken, aloud, in less than twenty minutes. It reads very convincingly, too. Let us, however, leave this point and return to a consideration of Amos's internal organization and structure.

In the previous chapter we discussed Amos's criticisms of the מִרְזַח. Here we will examine the textual unity of that section, Amos 6:1-10. The first seven verses of chapter 6 are a complex literary unit nicely knit together by the anaphoric use of the definite article beginning verses 3, 4, 5, and 6 (and echoing the interrogative הַ beginning verse 2). The use of יַיִן מִזְרָק קִי (verse 6) is a fine wordplay on מִזְרָה (and perhaps on מַרְבֵּק in verse 4) and further exemplifies the poetic devices with which the passage abounds. Other possible wordplays include the oft-noted רֵאשִׁית הַגּוֹיִם (verse 1) with בְּרֹאשׁ גּוֹלִים in verse 7 and, perhaps, רֵאשִׁת שְׁמָנִים in verse 6; even מֹצְאָן in verse 4 might be picking up צִיּוֹן in verse 1. (See discussion

---

[17]Thus Wolff, Mays, Cripps, Weiser, and Eissfeldt.

[18]The "corrections" of Psalm 119 by David Mueller are mentioned above.

[19]Johannes Lindblom, *Prophecy in Ancient Israel* (Philadelphia: Fortress, [2]1963) 241. But (243), "Apart from some minor additions, the Book of Amos has always had its present arrangement."

[20]Smalley, "Recursion Patterns," 122.

of Zion, above.) Surely, Amos's abilities as a poet indicate that so-called irregularities in the text may be intentional.

Similar observations have been made about the judicious use of vocabulary in the well-known poem of 3:3-8. What has not been seen is that, with the possible exception of verse 7 which also has its defenders (see note 21, below), the piece's seven rhetorical questions with anaphoric initial consonants followed by a responding "couplet" remind one of an English sonnet.

A more sustained composition based on a sevenfold exposition is found in 2:7–3:2. Amos accuses Israel of seven sins (2:7ff.). The indictment is followed by a sudden shift into first person that, again, most scholars see as proof of interpolated material.[11] They do not see that the following section consists of seven benefices that God has granted Israel and that a subsequent section (2:14-16) contains a sevenfold punishment for sin. In other words, the section in question is an organic whole.

Beginning in 2:9, Amos, with a fine disregard for chronology,[22] has God remind Israel that he

1. defeated the Amorites and
2. destroyed their history
3. and their posterity;
4. led Israel from Egypt;
5. accompanied Israel in the wilderness;
6. raised prophets from among her children and
7. (raised) Nazirites from her firstborn sons.

Those who insist on strict synonymous parallelism may object to my breaking "stereotyped" phrases[23] into component parts. Indeed, two of these phrases are good merisms, but that is not the way Amos is using them. His audience, I think, will have understood this list as seven good things done by God, just as they could read the preceding as seven sins and the following as a list of seven calamities.

---

[21]Not Yehoshua Gitay, "A Study of Amos's Art of Speech," CBQ 42 (1980): 305, nor Abraham Joshua Heschel, *The Prophets* (New York: Harper, 1962) 2:90 n.3, who brings a number of passages he feels are comparable.

[22]Given the amount of space Amos devotes to the subject, might he be referring to the Israelite invasions of Canaan both before and after the sojourn in Egypt?

[23]Ezra Zion Melamed, "Break-Up of Stereotype Phrases as an Artistic Device in Hebrew Poetry," SH 8 (12961): 115-44, allows scope for what I contend here.

Verses 2:14ff., like the first seven oracles, can be divided into groups of three, three, and one members respectively. We can also see them as a list of seven:

1. flight will fail the swift;
2. strength will not avail the strong;
3. wealth will not save the גִּבּוֹר;
4. the archer,
5. the infantry ("swift of foot"), and
6. the cavalry ("horsemen") will perish;
7. (even) the commander-in-chief (or bravest of the brave) will be forced to slink away.

Gordis was right to see "seven" as the key structural device in Amos.[24] But Amos has more strings in his bow.

What we regard as the first two verses of chapter 3 make a good peroration,[25] especially if it is aimed against the Northern Kingdom.[26]

> Hear this word, O people of Israel,
> That the Lord has spoken concerning you,
> Concerning the whole family that I brought up from the land of Egypt:
> You alone have I singled out
> Of all the families of the earth—
> That is why I will call you to account
> For all your iniquities.

And so he will do. The gifts of God are complete (seven); the sins of Israel are complete; the punishment will be complete. If Amos holds out any hope for a return he does not show it here. (I might add that the point of the above exposition is not to judge Amos's theology, but the book's unity.)

The first two verses of chapter 3 also set the tone for what follows, a portion of text knit together by five imperatives of שמע (3:1, 9, 13; 4:1;

---

[24]Robert Gordis, "The Heptad as an Element in Biblical and Rabbinic Style," JBL 62 (1943): 17.

[25]Coote recognizes this, *Amos among the Prophets,* 66. He puts it in the "B" stage of composition.

[26]B. Jongeling, "La Particule רַק," OTS 18 (1973): 97-107, informs us that *raq* is rare in prophets, but Samuel E. Loewenstamm, "The Address 'Listen' in the Ugaritic Epic and the Bible," in *The Bible World,* ed. Gary Rendsburg (New York: KTAV, 1980) 123-31, sees this passage as "ordinary speech" merely asking for attention. Gitay agrees ("Study," 294), saying, "The unity is in the whole, not the parts."

5:1) and the fivefold repetition "still you did not return to me" (4:6, 8, 9, 10, 11). To see just how pervasive is Amos's reuse of vocabulary, see Victor Maag's *Text, Wortshatz, und Begriffswelt des Buches Amos* (1951) and our next chapter below.

If there is one part of Amos that is universally considered nonunitary, it is the five visions in chapters 7–9. I do not think visions four and five are additions, as some scholars do. Nonetheless, it is apparent Amos wants us to consider the first three as a unit. Form, content, and placement tell us this. One could argue, as I have elsewhere, that differing forms are indirect proof of authenticity, and sets of five are almost as noticeable in Amos as sevens. Even so, I doubt the last two visions are of a piece with the first three, which are a discernible unit.

"Locusts" are a recurring natural hazard. God calls them back on appeal from Amos (7:1ff.) because "Jacob is so small." There is no need to read this literally, as Haran does,[27] indicating either geographical smallness or military weakness. Human frailty in the face of nature is a familiar biblical theme. (The Mormons in Utah had problems with locusts, too, and the locust swarm of 1988 in North Africa almost defies description.)

The second vision's "fire" is not (in this case) a natural disaster, but points to destruction in war. The kind of fire that destroys whole cities is likely to be that perpetrated by foreign armies, as Hammerschaimb thinks is the case in the oracles.[28] Amos reflects this with its use of "I will send fire . . . ," so reminiscent of Assyrian records such as the Kurkh Stele,[29] and of Hosea 8:14. However this may be, the fire-terror is called back after Amos intercedes (7:5)—Jacob is so small.

Note that both these terrors are external and therefore not under the control of those to whom they happen, the Israelites. The third is quite otherwise. The vision in 7:7ff., however one decides its grammatical prob-

---

[27]Menahem Haran, "The Rise and Decline of the Empire of Jeroboam ben Joash," VT 17 (1967): 278, maintains Jeroboam's expansion could only have taken place shortly before the rise of Tiglath-pileser III. Cf. Wolff, *Joel and Amos,* 164. On 348 Wolff gives a similar denotation to "house of Jacob." Does Amos address any of his remarks to non-Northerners? I think not.

[28]Hammerschaimb, *The Book of Amos,* 26.

[29]Kurkh Stele ii.87ff., translated in DOTT as "I set fire to his palaces." The same words are uttered by Elisha to Hazael in 2 Kgs 8:12. Is this, then, some sort of widely known annalistic formula?

lems,[30] measures the righteousness of Israelite society and finds it wanting.[31] If any appeal is to be made here, it will not be to God.

God may be relied upon to prevent natural disasters and foreign incursions, but only so long as Israel maintains Torah-true righteousness. Deuteronomy 11:13-17, with its promise of rain in due season as a reward for obedience, is still a regular part of Jewish weekly worship. When that righteous behavior ceases, as the previous chapters in Amos so graphically demonstrate, there is no longer any protection. The set of three visions ends with the statement that Jeroboam's dynasty will be overthrown "by the sword."

Whether this vision constitutes incitement to violence (as Elisha's words to Hazael) or a kind of desperate prediction,[32] it would certainly seem to qualify as a treasonous statement comparable to Micaiah ben Imlah's words to Ahab. It is not surprising, then, that just here Amaziah interrupts Amos with the command to stop.

In 1940 Robert Gordis could say, "All critics are agreed that it [Amos 7:10-17] is not in its proper place"; fifteen years later John D. W. Watts asserted, "There is every reason to agree that it is properly placed."[33] Cripps proposes[34] that 7:10-17 may have been inserted into a four-vision

---

[30]One problem is the lack of a subject in the first clause. See ad loc (BHK p. 924; BHS p. 1,025). (But ETT routinely presuppose the same formula as at 7:1, 4; 8:1—see, e.g., JB.)

[31]There is virtual agreement among all commentators on this point.

[32]Blenkinsopp, *History of Prophecy,* 23 and 91, claims, unconvincingly, that the "false" prediction of Jeroboam's violent death is the reason the "Deuteronomic historian" passes over Amos. On the problem of "false prophecy," see James L. Crenshaw, *Prophetic Conflict,* BZAW 124 (Berlin: de Gruyter, 1971) 13-22.

[33]Robert Gordis, "The Composition and Structure of Amos," HTR 33 (1940): 239. Karl Budde, "Zu Text und Auslesung des Buches Amos," JBL 44 (1925): 77, on the other hand, suggested "Dieser Bericht hat wahrscheinlich zunachst am Anfang des Buche seine Stelle gehabt." ["This account probably at first had its place at the beginning of the book."] John D. W. Watts, "The Origin of the Book of Amos," ET 66 (1954/1955): 109, agrees, but in *Vision and Prophecy in Amos,* 31ff., he straddles.

[34]Richard Cripps, *A Critical and Exegetical Commentary on the Book of Amos,* rev. ed. (London: S.P.C.K., 1955) 311. Gene Tucker, "Prophetic Authenticity. A Form-Critical Study of Amos 7:10-17," *Interpretation* 27 (1973): 425, assumes a unity of the five while Watts (*Vision and Prophecy,* 27-50) posits a 2 + 2 + 1 scheme, but does not deny "a common formula behind all five."

speech. Talmon[35] connects four of the visions with seasons mentioned in the Gezer Calendar, while Weiser[36] organizes the whole set around the second vision. Nor do these permutations exhaust the repertoire of scholarly suggestions. Is the section where it always was? We do not know, but by having 7:10-17 in its present place, the author generates a picture of events happening simultaneously, heightening the drama of the subsequent confrontation. Is it fanciful to suggest that Amaziah's interruption disrupted Amos's speech and thought patterns?

After predicting the utter ruin of the priest Amaziah and his family (in words reminiscent of treaty language) Amos goes on to relate something else God had shown him. Of course, it is by definition a vision, though not couched in exactly the same terms as the first three. But again the same argument that holds Amos to be knowledgeable of various speech forms holds here. Since he is an outraged citizen, not a professional prophet, and since he has just traded words with the priest, he is not too careful about continuing in exactly the same style as he employed before the interruption.

Seen in this light, Watts's clever reconstruction of the "hymn fragments" that Amos so carelessly scatters in his book becomes needless. Amos drives home his points using pieces of a hymn known to his audience. As Northrop Frye notes in the epigraph to this chapter, the twin purposes of rhetorical prose are "ornament and persuasion." It would hardly have helped Amos's cause if he had sung the whole hymn straight through.

If the text of Amos really were the product of many hands and several centuries, then its textual unevenness might indeed be cause for wonder. However, if it is largely what the man himself said, apparent irregularities may be deemed deliberate and not the result of errors in transmission. The only verse I think must be out of place is 5:3, because it reads so well with 6:9. But if so, how explain its apparent migration?

There is a "unity" to Amos's message as well. Doom is coming and the days shorten. Portents abound: 8:9 seems to refer to the eclipse of 763 B.C.E.; also see 4:11; 6:11; 7:7-8; 8:8; and 9:1.

Literarily, chapter 9 forms a many-sided *misgeret sifrutit* ("literary framework") with Amos's earlier words. For example, the use of נוּס and the roots מלט, פלט in 9:1 reminds hearers of 2:14-16; the five statements

---

[35]Shemaryahu Talmon, "The Gezer Calendar and the Seasonal Cycle of Ancient Canaan," JAOS 83 (1963): 177-87. Artur Weiser, *Die Prophetie von Amos*, BZAW 53 (Giessen: Topelmann, 1929) 13-14.

[36]Weiser, *Amos*, 13-14, obviously influencing Watts, who acknowledges it.

with עָם ("if they flee . . . ") recall the five questions in 3:3ff. or the other groups of five mentioned above. Carmel, unmentioned since 1:2, reappears in 9:3.[37]

Amos ends by suggesting that the Northern Kingdom stands no higher in God's estimation than any other people (9:7).[38] Or, rather, having failed to meet the high standards asked of her when she left Egypt, Israel is no longer of any more consequence and God can look upon her downfall and despair with equanimity. For, he says—and this must have been positively the last straw—God is redirecting his love and care to Judah (9:11ff.). The south—symbolized by the "fallen tabernacle of David"—will rise again.

Seen in this light, if 1:2 was added later it is not out of place. Amos's "Zion" is Jerusalem.

One may, I suppose, see Amos or a whole committee of people named "Amos" working throughout the centuries to polish this little bit of Scripture. If so, it is truly remarkable they made or allowed so many mistakes. I prefer to see and read it as the brief outpouring of one man's soul, and think it reads powerfully and well. This does not mean I accept the authenticity of every word and every verse without question.

Amos has favorite words,[39] and he uses all his words with great skill. I wish to suggest that only those verses contining at least three words— excluding proper names—none of which is found elsewhere in Amos should be considered suspect. The verses best fitting this description are 3:7; 4:13; 5:13; 5:25; and 9:13. There are others, namely, 4:9; 5:9; 5:26, but the first of these fits in its context while the latter two contain proper names.

Yehoshua Gitay[40] defends 3:7 as an intentional dramatic pause before the closing verse of 3:3-8. It may be so. Certainly, it constitutes an aside,

---

[37]But note the Hebrew behind 5:11's "delightful vineyards." Smalley, "Recursion Patterns," notices these things, as one would expect.

[38]It is not necessary, then, to decide whether Amos is "universalist" or "narrowly nationalist" in outlook. My interpretation inclines toward the latter because Amos is a patriot, not a prophet. Coote, *Amos among the Prophets,* 66, also reads 3:1-2 with the preceding.

[39]E.g., אַרְמֹנוֹת. See ch. 7, p. 91. Amos uses הֵיכָל only once (8:3). Why does he prefer one to the other?

[40]Gitay, "Study," 305. H. H. Rowley, "Was Amos a *Nabi?*" in *Festschrift für Otto Eissfeldt,* ed. Johann Fück (Halle: Niemeyer, 1947) 194, does not reject it, though most scholars do not agree. See Irwin, "Thinking," 105, or James L. Mays, *Amos. A Commentary* (Philadelphia: Westminster, 1969) 137. Blenkinsopp, *History,* 89, terms it "the most obvious Deuteronomic interpolation in Amos."

if not an interruption. And it contains three words—גָּלָה "reveal," סוֹדוֹ "(his) secret," and עֲבָדָיו "(his) servant(s)"—not found elsewhere. סוֹד, by the way, is considered a Wisdom term; its loss from Amos would weaken Wolff's case, but the point here is only that, suddenly, Amos uses vocabulary not found elsewhere and the passage reads just as well without this verse as with it.

There is enormous danger in rejecting text for so-called stylistic reasons. This arbitrarily assumes all speakers and writers of biblical texts were confined to some one style, mode, or genre of expression. It conduces toward various reductionisms in a sort of self-fulfilling prophecy by substituting our idea of consistency for theirs. And it requires the invention of those tendentious editors and sleepy copyists, each of whom had exclusive access to the one single "Bureau-of-Standards text" that, moreover, no one else even knew orally.

Still, we know that texts, oral or written, were not static. I think 3:7 is not original. The hymn fragments are probably not "original" either, but only in the sense they are probably quoted from another piece.[41] On the other hand, 5:3 seems to be original, though possibly out of place. I am not sure about 5:25[42] or 9:13. Weiser[43] thought the latter an even later addition than most of the other additions. I maintain it could refer to Judah. For the rest, given the probable circumstances of Amos's original irruption, I cannot with certainty exclude anything else after the superscription. But perhaps we should not finally decide this question without first looking at the astonishing breadth and provenance of Amos's vocabulary. This is the subject of the next chapter.

---

[41]"[Q]uotations would be particularly congenial to the *hakam,* who, unlike the prophet, lays no claim to direct supernatural revelation, but depends on careful and patient observation and logical deductions." Robert Gordis, "Quotations as a Literary Usage in Biblical, Oriental, and Rabbinic Literature," HUCA 22 (1949): 165. Thirty percent of the passages Gordis lists (189) are from Psalms.

[42]Cf. 5:8-9. Are these common nouns or proper names? Stanley Gevirtz, "A New Look at an Old Crux, Amos 5:26," JBL 84 (1965): 267-76, translates "shrine of your (god) MLK" (276). If so, 9:11 "shrine/booth of David" is probably a conscious wordplay and, of course, original. G. R. Driver, "Astronomical," 208-209, retrieves a fine suggestion of G. Hoffmann's identifying the troublesome nouns in 5:8-9 as constellations, but Lawrence Zalcman, "Astronomical Illusions in Amos," JBL 100 (1981): 53-58, refutes it.

[43]Artur Weiser, *The Old Testament. Its Formation and Development,* trans. D. M. Barton (New York: Association, 1961) 245.

Before addressing that subject, however, it would be well to recapitulate.

The main line of Jewish and Christian tradition has always assumed Amos was a Judean because (a) the Tekoa we know is in the South, (b) he was "anti-Northern," (c) we are all unconscious heirs of Judah, not Samaria, and (d) Amos's message made his birthplace seem insignificant.

Critics of the mainline position have cavilled about this or that aspect and seen a series of small things that have made them uncomfortable: Amos's knowledge and articulateness, his comparatively mild treatment by the Northern establishment, the absence of sycamores in Tekoa. Some few have even suggested Amos was not from Judah. No one, however, has hypothesized that most if not all the problems associated with our traditional understanding of the text of Amos are solved by positing a Northern origin.

But consider, if Amos is a Northern government official—not a recognized prophet—who is inspired to pronounce judgment against his own kingdom, he will (a) produce a corpus of writings somewhat eclectic in style that (b) will be "canonized" shortly after what he predicts comes to pass, and, therefore, (c) will largely escape the editorial activities we see in other parts of the Judeans' scripture. (Note that Amos and the fictional Jonah are the only two minor prophets whose position in the canon differs between Massoretic and Septuagint traditions.)

The text we have is not without its problems, but the underlying structure based on clusters of seven (or five) things, the use and reuse of vocabulary, especially in 3:3-8 and 6:1-10, the extensive literary framework that connects chapter 9 with chapter 1, and the many wordplays that dot the text all point to a single author of considerable skill. Moreover, depending upon the rate of delivery and audience interruptions beyond that mentioned in chapter 7, the whole speech could be delivered in about twenty minutes.

There is no compelling reason, then, for assuming the present text to be anything but largely authentic and the work of its traditional author.

7

Languages and Dialect in Amos

Les mots ont une âme; la plupart des lecteurs et même des écrivains ne leur demandent qu'un sens. Il faut trouver cette âme qui apparait au contact d'autres mots. . . .   —Guy de Maupassant

The title of this chapter reflects the variety of "languages" scholars have found in Amos. As we have seen, Wolff's Amos owes to "wisdom"; to Farr the source is "cultic"; Crenshaw looks for "theophanic" language; while Brueggemann prefers "covenantal." Würthwein extols "apodictic law"; Gottwald looks to "pre-Israelite prophecy"; and Kapelrud thinks Psalms was a major influence on *Amos*.[1] Not surprisingly, Mays commends Amos for his versatility.[2]

Are we really prepared to see so many influences at work in so brief a text? Isn't this, rather, the all-too-familiar use of Scripture-as-Rorschach-test? Surprisingly, in the case of Amos, it is possible to see all these influences at work. If he was a well-placed and well-off member of the Northern Kingdom's bureaucracy, it not only allows Amos to show all the influences scholars have seen in the text, but even accounts for the eclectic use of so many different traditional sources. The burden of this chapter,

---

[1]Walter Brueggemann, "Amos 4:4-13 and Israel's Covenant Worship," VT 15 (1965): 1-15. James L. Crenshaw, "Amos and the Theophanic Tradition," ZAW 80 (1968): 203-15. The works of Farr, Kapelrud, Wolff, and Gottwald are listed below, in the bibliography.

[2]James Luther Mays, *Amos. A Commentary* (Philadelphia: Westminster, 1969) 6.

however, is to investigate Amos from a point of view that has only recently been assayed—that represented by the study of Hebrew dialect.

Before sailing into these poorly charted waters, however, I must enter a caveat. This chapter cannot offer proof that Amos was a Northerner; questions of language and text transmission do not allow such certainty. I hope the preceding chapters have already moved readers to consider seriously that Amos may have been a native of Israel and that he—rather than "scribal tradition"—is responsible for the text we have in pretty much the shape it is in now. In that case it is worth looking at that text to see what *additional* support for the theory may be gleaned from examining it.

That there should be dialects in biblical Hebrew is no surprise. It would be more surprising if there were none. However, the famous "shibboleth incident" of Judges 12:6 is some proof that dialects of Hebrew existed from at least the period of the Conquest.[3] After that time, the situation with regard to Hebrew dialects will have gotten more complex: as Garr reminds us, the topography of Israel conduces to the isolation of its various communities.[4] Yet despite the large number of strange forms and of rare and foreign words and spellings in Amos, none of the standard commentaries[5] has suggested that what we have here is more comprehensive if its author is a Northerner. Whatever else it is, the language of Amos is one that betrays Northern influences.

There are at least two reasons for scholars paying so little attention to this aspect of the text. The first is that we cannot prove our text records Amos's exact words. Rashi,[6] of course, thinks it does, but the many irreg-

[3]Ephraim A. Speiser's treatment of "The Shibboleth Incident" (in *Oriental and Biblical Studies,* ed. Moshe Greenberg and J. J. Finkelstein [Philadelphia: University of Pennsylvania Press, 1967] 143-50) has been criticized, e.g., by Eduard Y. Kutscher, *A History of the Hebrew Language* (Jerusalem: Magnes, 1982) 14, and Joshua Blau,·" 'Weak' Phonetic Change and the Hebrew SIN," HAR 1 (1977): 67-120, esp. 108-109. No one, however, denies there were dialects in Hebrew. See below, n.18.

[4]W. Randall Garr, *Dialect Geography of Syria-Palestine, 1000–586 BCE* (Philadelphia: University of Pennsylvania Press, 1985) 7.

[5]James Davila's contribution to the forthcoming Segert Festschrift will contain his paper "Qoheleth and Northern Hebrew," presented to the SBL Northwest Semitic Epigraphy Group at the AAR/SBL annual meeting in Atlanta, November 1986, on Northern influences in Qoheleth. My thanks to him for providing me a manuscript copy.

[6]Rashi (Rabbi Solomon ben Isaac, 11th-century French exegete) ad loc 7:14, cited by Lawrence Zalcman, "Piercing the Darkness at *bôqēr,*" VT 30 (1980): 254.

ularities bother him so much he is forced to posit that Amos had a speech impediment! For all his own cleverness, Rashi lived nearly 2,000 years after Amos: Who could take him seriously?[7]

The second reason is the assumption that, like so many other biblical books, this one went through many editorial changes so recovering what is "authentic" Amos, let alone the words in which he himself cast it, lies in the misty realm of sheer guesswork. Not that scholars let such considerations impede us. . . .

Harper typifies the modern scholar's lack of interest in "lower criticism" by his guessing that the "misspellings are all textual errors."[8] This would seem to rule out the use of a scribe—a competent scribe, anyway— but can Harper and other moderns really expect us to believe that the same editors who cleverly inserted their own concerns into prophetic texts failed, generation by generation, to correct spellings until the "tradition" ruled they were no longer free to do so? Think of הֹי־הֹו in 5:16, followed by הֹי in 5:18 and 6:1.

Gunkel holds[9] that copyists were not at liberty to change what they had in front of them, so when were the errors made? If parts of Amos were postexilic and if the corpus of "Prophets" was considered canonical by 450 B.C.E.,[10] there is precious little time for the text to have attained its present, crabbed form. We should have to posit that a text that had been fluid for more than 200 years suddenly set hard in less than two generations. Not likely. Further, we know from rabbinic sources that some cor-

---

[7]Zalcman himself, ibid., guesses that "Amos's pronunciation of Hebrew may have been preserved at various points in the text." This is congruent with my own theory that the text of Amos was, as it were, "quick-frozen."

[8]William Rainey Harper, *A Critical and Exegetical Commentary on Amos and Hosea,* ICC (Edinburgh: T. & T. Clark, 1905) cxxxviii. Ernst Würthwein, *The Text of the Old Testament* (Oxford: Blackwell, 1962) 71, cautions, "this assumption should be made as rarely as possible."

[9]As cited by John Willis, "Redaction Criticism and Historical Reconstruction," in *Encounter with the Text,* ed. Martin Buss (Philadelphia: Fortress, 1979) 85. The rabbinic system that safeguards texts against errors in transmission is well known. How early did it start?

[10]For those who assume that only one authorized copy of each book existed at any one time, e.g., Martin-Archard and Re'emi, ten minutes would be enough. Norman H. Snaith, *Amos, Hosea, and Micah* (London: Epworth, 1956), brings the date of canonization down to 280 B.C.E., leaving more time for errors but not explaining why they should persist.

rections of biblical texts, the *Tikkune Sophrim,* did take place.[11] But there is no evidence of that activity here in Amos.[12] Surely, few people would have objected to such changes as regularizing spellings—"Isaac," for example (see below)—or changing such "wrong" pronominal suffixes as 4:1's הֶם for כֶּם,[13] unless these variations are not mistakes but rather recognizable dialect forms. (Compare Southern U.S.A. "y'all" and Northeastern U.S.A. "youse.")

Elsewhere,[14] Harper mentions that Judah and Israel may have had differences in dialect, but does not see this admission as at odds with his previous statement. Of course, Harper wrote at the turn of the century. It remained for later scholars, principally Zellig Harris and Alexander Sperber, to explore the ramifications.[15]

Sperber's ambitious work postulates that Hebrew contained a major dialect in each kingdom.[16] Harris thinks the dialect boundaries were becoming fixed in Amos's time.[17] As though anticipating Garr's remark (note 4 above) about local communication, Harris sees a "local, non-Jerusalemite dialect" in the Gezer Calendar.[18] Gezer is barely a stone's throw from Jerusalem. How much more so, then, may we suppose the many strange features of the text of Amos are not careless errors at all, but evidence for its Northern provenance.

What is this evidence? I divide it into three parts: spelling, foreign words, and peculiar forms.

The most astonishing of the many "misspellings" in Amos is the name "Isaac," spelled יִשְׂחָק in 7:9, 16. The same spelling is found in Jeremiah

---

[11]See EncJud 15:1,139-40 for a brief discussion and list.

[12]Michael Fishbane, *Biblical Interpretation in Ancient Israel* (London: Oxford University Press, 1985) 40-41, notes no deictic activity here.

[13]Gary Rendsburg, "Evidence for a Spoken Hebrew in Biblical Times" (Ph.D. diss., New York University, 1980) 28 passim, uses these forms among his "proofs."

[14]Harper, *Amos and Hosea,* 45. Later (167) he cites earlier studies as recognizing provincialisms in language. See below, n.18.

[15]Zellig S. Harris, *Development of the Canaanite Dialects,* AOS 16 (New Haven CT: Yale University Press, 1939) and Alexander Sperber, *A Historical Grammar of Biblical Hebrew* (Leiden: E. J. Brill, 1966).

[16]Sperber, *Grammar,* 105ff.

[17]Harris, *Development,* 96.

[18]Ibid., 24. Kutscher (*History,* 55) writes, "It is perhaps no mere chance that מוֹצָא can be pinpointed only in the region of Jerusalem." See also Jonas Greenfield, "Dialect Traits in Early Aramaic," *Lesonenu* 32 (1960): 359-68.

33:9 and Psalms 105:9. Surely, these cannot all be dismissed as "textual errors." If so, we should have to ask, Why the same error in all four verses? Jerome remarks on the pronunciation of **צ** and the "noncommittal sigma" used overwhelmingly in the LXX to transliterate it. But no one who knew Hebrew would back-translate יִשְׂחָק,[19] so it cannot come from the versions. It is more likely that, since the three texts (Amos, Jeremiah, and Psalm 105) may all be presumed to have Northern parentage (Jeremiah's family was from the North), the alternate spellings could be a dialect variant.

Further proof of this may be adduced from a comparison of Psalm 105:1-15 with its doublet in 1 Chronicles 16:8-22. This pair of texts manifests two interesting differences. One is a change (?) to "Israel" (as a parallel with Jacob in 1 Chr 16:13) from "Abraham" in Psalm 105:6, the other a change from יִשְׂחָק (Ps 105:9) to יִצְחָק in 1 Chronicles 16:16. One's view of the Chronicler's politics might decide whether "Israel" (often used of the Northern Kingdom alone) or "Abraham" is the original word, but only a desire to regularize pronunciation will account for the change in the spelling of "Isaac."[20] Why was this not done in the Amos texts and Jeremiah? Probably because, unlike Psalms, they were not used for liturgical purposes.

Writing about the shibboleth incident, A. F. L. Beeston concludes that

in Ephraimite, realisation [*sic*!] of . . . *šblt* must have been precluded by the lack in that dialect of *š* . . . [21]

Or as Zeev Ben-Hayyim puts it, "a Samaritan commentator is entitled to see the roots *š-ḥ-t* and *ś-ḥ-t* as one root."[22] If Amos's dialect were "Ephraimite," that could explain many of his book's anomalies.

---

[19]Cited by Sperber, *Grammar*, 367, who explains that "the obelus *group* of the Hexaplaric LXX" derives from a Samarian tradition. (Italics in original.) E. A. Speiser, "The Pronunciation of Hebrew," JQR 23 (1933): 254, had earlier drawn attention to Origen's use of Σ for **צ**.

[20]Sperber (ibid.) suggests, "we may be justified in ascribing the Tiberian way of differentiating between שׁ and שׂ to the Judean dialect." It is possible, therefore, to back-translate a Σ (for original **צ**) to שׂ but not, I think, in the name Isaac.

[21]Alfred Beeston, "Hebrew *šibbolet* and *sobel*," JSS 24 (1979): 175. I am indebted to Edd Rowell who pointed out here the British "realisation" as opposed to the American spelling with 'z'. A fortiori, then, the differences between Hebrew dialects.

[22]Zeev Ben-Hayyim, *The Literary and Oral Tradition of Hebrew and Aramaic amongst the Samaritans*, vol. 4 (Jerusalem: Academy of Hebrew Language, 1977) 113. Similarly, N. H. Tur-Sinai, *Job. A New Commentary* (Jerusalem: Kiriath-Sepher, 1957) 38-45, feels Hebrew שָׂטַן derives from an original סָטַן.

The most important of these, as we indicated in chapter 4, was the hapax legomenon בּוֹלֵס שִׁקְמִים. To reiterate what was said there, the phrase
has been read as a kind of confirmation of Amos's humble station by connecting בּוֹלֵס with Ethiopic *b-l-s* "gash" or "scratch." However, since
Wright informs us[23] that Palestinian sycamore figs do not need gashing in
order to ripen, the Ethiopic cognate is less appropriate, perhaps, than Targumic Aramaic בָּלָשׁ, "searcher," "constable."[24] Hence, our contention
that Amos might have been a government official, one of whose duties was
the oversight of sycamores in a given administrative district.

If Ephraimite Hebrew did not possess the שׂ phoneme, then Amos's
compatriots would not say בּוֹלֵס any more than their ancestors would have
said שְׁבוֹלֶת. There are other traces of the same sort of confusion in Amos,[25]
and, while none of them occur with sufficient frequency to allow conclu-
sions, they may conduce to a new appreciation for the extent of sibilant
confusion between and among the various dialects of Hebrew. Amos is
tantalizingly inconsistent, as in the two spellings of "Damascus" (שׂ in
chapter 1 and in 5:27, but שׂ in 3:12), and the two spellings—or are they
two different words?—רצץ in 4:1 and רסס in 6:11. But this very incon-
sistency speaks for the essential authenticity of the present text of Amos.

We might now return to a similar concern mentioned earlier,[26] the appearance of "Zion" in 6:1. Most commentators take it as evidence for the
catholicity of Amos's concerns; H. L. Ginsberg doesn't and emends it to
בְּיוֹסֵף ("in Joseph," the tribe of Ephraim west of the Jordan and Manasseh, mostly east of the river). Granted Amos is not primarily concerned
with the fate of the other countries, is Ginsberg's emendation necessary?

The spelling of "zion" is variable. We know from Deuteronomy 3:9
that the Phoenicians called Mt. Hermon שִׂרְיֹן (with ס not שׂ), the same
name it bears in the Northern poem we know as Psalm 29, but which in
Deuteronomy 4:48 is spelled שִׂיאֹן.

---

[23]Wright's observations are found in ch. 4, above.

[24]Morris Jastrow, *A Dictionary of the Targumim, the Talmud Babli and Yerushalmi, and the Midrashic Literature* (New York: Pardes, 1950) 1:175. Franz Rosenthal, *A Grammar of Biblical Aramaic* (Wiesbaden: Harrassowitz, 1963) 16, suggests
there was already in biblical Aramaic an "incipient" change from שׂ to ס.

[25]E.g., בּוֹשַׂסְכֶם in 5:11. Most commentators make it from בשׂ but N. H Tur-
Sinai (then Harry Torczyner), in his "Presidential Address," JPOS 16 (1936): 6-
7, connects it with Akkadian *šabašu* (= "be angry with," "mistreat"). BHS (but
not BHK) in the apparatus suggests emending שְׁבִי in 4:10 to צְבִי "beauty." These
are all akin to trace elements in chemistry, but what are they traces of?

[26]See above, p. 30.

"Zion," then, is not a particular spot, but the place that one's tradition associates with God's primary dwelling.[27] In Canaan's pre-Israelite past it was most likely Mt. Hermon, Mt. Carmel, Mt. Tabor, or all three. For us it has been Jerusalem, but for most Northerners in 760 B.C.E. it was probably Beth El and/or Samaria (with Shechem's Mt. Gerizim as another possibility). In any event, if the spelling of this word could employ either a fricative or nonfricative sibilant,[28] then צִיּוֹן in Amos 6:1 is a perfectly proper *Northern* parallel to Samaria in the same verse. Since Amos employs the "Judean" spelling, we have to posit that (a) he used the Southern pronunciation, perhaps as a challenge to his hearers, or (b) here is a rare change that has crept into the Amos-text.

Amos's own name might have had more than one spelling as well. Ephraim Speiser claims[29] that א and ע were pronounced the same in some northern parts of Israel—though he doesn't tell us the period during which this obtained. Is it possible our prophet and Isaiah's father have the same name, might even be the same person? To forget so important a connection seems well-nigh inconceivable; I do not insist on it. My point is to suggest that future scholarly work on the frontiers of dialect variation might yield surprising results.

A second area of linguistic interest is the many foreign loan words or forms in Amos. The most well know of these, of course, is אֲנָךְ "tin" or "lead" (or "uranium"!)[30] in 7:7-8; the translation does not matter. What matters is that Amos is the only biblical author to use this word. Surely, this usage, with the many others we will shortly see, tells against the notion that he was a rustic, Judean or otherwise.

Other important words with foreign cognates found in Amos include בַּרְזֶל "iron," which, though common enough in Scripture, is found only in Amos and Micah among the minor prophets; אַרְמוֹנוֹת, which the Book

---

[27]With Peters and Fohrer, above, p. 33.

[28]See Richard C. Steiner, *Affricated Ṣade in the Semitic Languages* (New York: American Academy for Jewish Research, 1982) 40.

[29]Speiser, "Pronunciation," 237, on the basis of TB Erubin 53 says, "א, ע, and ח were all pronounced alike north of the valley of the Jezreel." He does not tell us how early this is attested. Jerome's difficulty with ע and ח is cited by Sperber, *Grammar*, 109-10.

[30]Thus Gilbert Brunet, "La Vision de l'étain: reinterpretation d'Amos 7:7-9," VT 16 (1966): 387-95. Better is William Holladay, "Once More 'Anak = Tin, Amos 7:7," VT 20 (1970): 492-94. Also Benno Landsberger, "Tin and Lead—the Adventures of Two Vocables," JNES 24 (1965): 285-96.

of Amos uses more times than the rest of the prophets combined; the oldest use of the rare (seven times) Akkadian loanword אִכָּר "husbandman" (5:16); and the Phoenician (?) words מִרְזַח[31] (found again only in Jer 16:5), בּוֹקֵר, and נֹקֵד.

The last three words may not be strictly Phoenician as they have widespread cognates elsewhere, but the Amos-text as a whole is rich in foreign terms appropriate to citizens of Israel's cosmopolitan Northern Kingdom. A political rupture may have accompanied Jezebel's death, but Phoenician influence would not have stopped.[32] This may be seen in Amos's use of the Pheonician *yiphil* verb form לַשְׁבִּית (8:4) for the expected לְהַשְׁבִּית.[33]

There may be a connection, too, between Phoenician and Northern Hebrew with regard to the first-person-singular pronoun. Scholars note the presence in Hebrew of two forms of "I" (אֲנִי and אָנֹכִי). Most suggest the long form was earlier or "poetic" or both, but Sperber informs us that אָנֹכִי was the preferred form in the Northern Kingdom.[34] Davila adds[35] that the long form is cognate with Phoenician *a-n-k*. It is not surprising, then, that Amos uses אָנֹכִי almost exclusively—eleven times, versus only one use (4:6) of the short form.[36] A similar situation is present in Deuteronomy where the longer form is preferred by a margin of ten to one over the shorter.[37]

---

[31]אִכָּר is identified as Sumerian by Kutscher, *History*, 50. It is used only seven times in Scripture, three of the seven in Jeremiah.

[32]Harris, *Development*, 98, proposes that the Northern Kingdom accepted many words from Phoenician that the South did not. If John Bright is correct (*A History of Israel* [Philadelphia: Westminster, 1972] 249 and passim), the South's isolation and relative religious conservatism are partly responsible for this difference.

[33]Stanislav Segert, *A Grammar of Phoenician and Punic* (Munich: Beck, 1976) 142-43, contra Rendsburg (n.13 above).

[34]Sperber, *Grammar*, 294; Garr, *Dialect Geography*, 79, agrees. Rendsburg (n.13 above), predictably, reads the long form as more evidence for a spoken form of Hebrew, but that a longer form should take precedence over a shorter one in spoken language defies common sense.

[35]Davila, "Qoheleth" (n.5 above) 6, notes it is also preferred in Punic. Is there a kind of provincial language conservatism operating there and in Israel?

[36]Hans Walter Wolff, *Joel and Amos*, Hermeneia (Philadelphia: Fortress, 1977) 213, observes that 4:6's use of אֲנִי is unique in Amos and thinks it an addition to the text. He does not use the same logic to deny authenticity to 8:3 even though only there does Amos use הֵיכָל rather than אַרְמוֹנוֹת.

[37]Hans Bauer and Pontus Leander, *Historische Grammatik der hebräischen Sprache des Alten Testaments* (Hildesheim: Olms, 1961, [1]1922) 249.

Table 4 shows the distribution of the two forms throughout a selection of books.

Table 4.   **Distribution (Selected Books) of אָנֹכִי and אֲנִי**

LOC CIT	אָנֹכִי	אֲנִי
Amos	11	1[1]
Deuteronomy	50+[2]	5+
Ruth	7	2
Joshua	9	4
Hosea	11	11
Micah	1	2
1 Isaiah	63	13
2 Isaiah	13	6
Jeremiah	35	50
Job	14	28
Chronicles	1	30
Ezekiel	1	160+

[1]The one use of אֲנִי in Amos 4:6 is held by many—e.g., Wolff, *Joel and Amos*, 213—to be secondary!

[2]The exact number will depend upon whether one counts forms with prepositions. In any case, the proportion remains about the same.

The wider implications of this table should be apparent. If we find a number of items whose distribution in various books is skewed, we may be justified in questioning whether the skewing is a function of dialect—as it is with regard to various forms of the second-person pronoun in different regions of the United States—not just "poetry." Such a study is well beyond the goal of the present work; however, a few observations are pertinent here.

Hosea provides a striking contrast. That prophet, in BHK or BHS, the text most of us use, employs each form an equal number of times. Since everyone admits Hosea's Northern origin, we may ask how this difference can be accounted for. The logical answer, as we indicated in the chapter on Amos's profession, is that Amos was not a prophet. His words, then, were not subject to the same "handling" as Hosea's and hence have come down to us in a form closer to the original. In this connection, we already observed[38] that *pesiq,* a scribal notation that seems to indicate some kind of external editing, is found eight times in Hosea, but only twice in Amos, both within the first two verses. There is little evidence for deictic changes in Amos.

---

[38]Above, n.12.

(This might also account for Hosea's being at the head of the minor prophets though Amos is chronologically prior.)

Deuteronomy's overwhelming preference for the long form might be explained in much the same way. Presumably, the ur-text corpus was insulated from editorial changes during the decades it lay unused in Jerusalem. This essay cannot do justice to that book's history, but our observation tells against the recent contention that Jeremiah wrote Deuteronomy.[39]

More merit attaches to Davila's speculation concerning Qoheleth, namely, that he lived in Jerusalem, as he himself claims, but continued to write "in his own rustic dialect."[40] A similar argument may be made for Amos on the basis of הַפֹּרְטִים in 6:5 and מְסָרְפוֹ in 6:10. The former is a Samarian word noted already by James Montgomery in 1906.[41] No one, apparently, has found it strange that Amos availed himself of what, to a Judean, would be a foreign term. It is true that Amos is here criticizing Samarians, but this word is found nowhere else in Scripture.

מְסָרְפוֹ is the subject of some controversy. NJB calls the Hebrew unintelligible and follows LXX, but G. R. Driver finds a Samarian burial term, *sk,* glossed here.[42] The similarity between שרף and סרף is striking; NJPST translates "who is to burn incense for him." Given its context, the activities of the *marzeah,* this should not be at all surprising. It indicates, again, that the Northern Kingdom could use ס in places Judeans use שׁ—or other sibilants—with the possibility of differing pronunciation from region to region.

By themselves, linguistic arguments of the sort presented here cannot be conclusive. It is just possible that Amos was a Southerner who resided in Israel long enough to have acquired or consciously adopted a "Northern accent." This is unlikely. I recall my grandfather, raised in Macon, Georgia, who kept his Southern accent through the forty-one years he lived in Chicago. More to the point, think of St. Peter's difficulty in Jerusalem,

---

[39]Richard Elliott Friedman, *Who Wrote the Bible?* (New York: Summit, 1987). Of Northern ancestry, Jeremiah might retain Northern diction, but his scribe Baruch ben-Neriah was a Southerner writing for Judeans. Baruch could be expected to write in his own Southern dialect without bothering to ask leave.

[40]Davila, "Qoheleth" (n.5 above) 22.

[41]James Montgomery, "Notes from the Samaritan," JBL 25 (1906): 51-52. Amos contains eight other hapax legomena, including the three we have remarked on.

[42]G. R. Driver, "A Hebrew Burial Custom," ZAW 66 (1954): 314-15. Joshua Blau, "On Pseudo-Corrections in Some Semitic Languages," *Israel Academic Journal of Sociology and History* (1970): 118, does not see the ס as secondary. Prof. Pardee informs me that some have read this word in Lachish Ostraca 6:8.

denying, in his Galilean accent, that he was one of Jesus' followers. (The detail concerning Peter's problem occurs only in Matthew, presumably because that book is aimed at a Jewish audience who would appreciate it.)

Or, again, Amos might have had some Northern "Baruch" whom no one remembers to write his words down for him. Still, added to the other arguments that have been made here, the weight of the linguistic evidence points the other way. If the text betrays a Northern origin, the most likely reason is that its author/speaker was a Northerner.

8

Conclusions
and Preamble to Further Study

How long will you judge perversely, showing favor to the wicked?
—Psalm 82:2*

If Amos was not the first of the Southern literary prophets, then he was the last of the Northern line and it is his text—and perhaps his person—which, along with Hosea, may be supposed to have brought the phenomenon of prophecy to the South. This possibility invites us to reconsider the entire history of Israelite prophecy, North and South.

Even before such a project were begun, I would urge we make a greater effort to consider each of the prophets separately and not rush to hack the message of "the prophets" from the circumstances in which each was first uttered. Admittedly, this is no easy task, because most of the prophetic books do show some evidence of editorial activity beyond the date of the first speaker. Still, not to attempt historical reconstruction as a background for each prophet's words because of the textual difficulty is to concede that the prophets can speak only to us, not to their own times.

It follows that we should be equally wary of writing those "histories of prophecy" that have always been a staple of modern Bible criticism. Unquestionably, Isaiah and Jeremiah and Joel are influenced by Amos, but

---

*[Editor's note. The original epigraph to this concluding chapter warrants canonization, if only here, in the textual apparatus. *Biblical scholarship is a form of worship undertaken by those who cannot sing.* —Ned Rosenbaum.]

it is a long jump from that statement to the assertion that anyone who comes later in the prophetic corpus knows and depends upon everyone who comes earlier. What we call the prophetic tradition is, really, the often very brief utterances (for instance, Obadiah) of perhaps two dozen scattered individuals, plus unnamed disciples, such prophets as Huldah who are mentioned in other texts but have left none of their own, and unremembered others who inhabit 300 to 600 years in Israel's long history. How much of the prophetic "tradition" each scriptural prophet consciously carried is a difficult question to answer. Our reconstructions often produce a more homogenized mixture than I suspect was originally the case.

Similarly, I hope to have shown that the sociology of Israel is both more knowable and therefore more relevant than we have previously realized. In our haste to mine moral messages from the words of these earliest social critics, we have thrown away a good deal of ore-bearing text. Even—no, especially—if the texts have been seriously edited, we need to assay what weight their words had in the period(s) in which they are used. This, too, is a time-consuming process and even in an age of computer-speed research may not strike gold. But the attempt has to be essayed.

A further result of this study should be more attempts to identify isoglosses and so define the limits of Hebrew dialects. It is not enough to concede that there were dialects and then not use that information. With due caution we might ultimately posit more precise regional origins for texts that give evidence of relatively coherent use of dialectical Hebrew. This should, in turn, give us greater insight into the process by which the Bible was formed.

Already we recognize psalms written for and in the Northern Kingdom: Psalm 82, quoted above, was doubtless known to Amos; and the core of Deuteronomy is acknowledged to be Israelite as well. How much more Northern influence will we find? And how did it make its way into the canon our Judean forebears collected?

The fault for the present state of affairs lies partly with our present set of tools. Just as looking at the world through a magnifying glass makes some objects clearer and others unrecognizable, so too the undiscriminating use of scholarly tools on all sorts of biblical texts produces better re-- sults for some than for others.

The present study suggests that in the case of Amos two critical assumptions—that Amos was a prophet and that his book was influenced by "Deuteronomic redaction"—have produced predictable results. Is it really necessary at this late date to say that the Documentary Hypothesis has *lim-*

ited value or that certain current dogmas of scholarship can be just as constraining as those that modern scholarship was called into being to combat?

I am aware that the time in which I live and write may have some bearing upon my "findings." For one thing, I share the Western conceit that a hypothesis that answers the most questions and leaves the fewest loose ends is thereby trustworthy. I am reminded of Dmitry Ivanovich Mendeleyev. In constructing the periodic table of the elements he found some were "missing," but he was confident they would eventually be discovered. And so they were.

Here is my reconstruction of Amos.

Amos was born around 800 B.C.E. into a Northern Kingdom family of some status. He had a quick mind and probably benefitted from better-than-average training. In time he entered the Israelite "civil service" where he rose to the rank of district inspector of government herds and of sycamores.

This was a time of relative prosperity in Israel because a reawakened Assyria, mindful of Israel's loyal vassalage, was again able to put pressure on Israel's hated rival, Aram. Indeed, Israel was able to reclaim some of the territory across the Jordan that had previously been lost. At the same time Israel put down an ill-conceived challenge from Judah, capturing the Southern king and even raiding Jerusalem.

But if times were good in Israel, they were good for some, not for all. The Jehu dynasty had provided stability, but its adherents battened on the land. Crown lands and army veterans' estates grew while peasant holdings shrank. Free for a while from Aramean incursions, Israel discovered that its wine and olive oil were sought-after commodities; a robust and rapacious capitalism was the first result.

Capitalism collapsed the country's vaunted—and perhaps mythical—egalitarianism. Lamentably, when Israel got a king "like the nations," she became just another Levantine autocracy. The gulf between rich and poor widened and with disparity in wealth came a greater-than-ever disparity in social class.

The affluent, those who controlled the organs of government and religion, maintained exclusive social/religious organizations in which all manner of excess, including imported cult prostitution, was encouraged. All this cost money, but of money there was seemingly no lack. Landless or luckless peasants provided a plentiful supply extorted from them in any number of ways, legal and otherwise.

Those freeholders who had the temerity to oppose exploitation had little recourse since the system of Israelite justice was itself for sale to the wealthy. Indeed, anyone who felt a twinge of compassion might be well advised to shut up about it.

Enter Amos.

Amos was a member of the "haves," but he felt for those less fortunate. Though he himself was a beneficiary of the system, the whole thing made him uncomfortable. He knew the system was rotten and that this was not the first time the Northern government had deviated from the true path of righteousness. His boyhood had been filled with tales of Elijah and Elisha, the latter but recently dead.

How long Amos brooded over his country's turpitude we do not know. Nor do we know whether he nerved himself to denounce his peers by practicing various formulations as he made his official rounds. Whatever the *preparatio,* he ultimately gave public vent to his passion, cleverly putting the audience on his side by criticizing some of Israel's neighbors before launching the attack on his own country.

The effect was electric. No one dared stop him. He was himself an Israelite official and he spoke in their own rich Northern tones. And he claimed to speak in God's name as well, giving him a sort of "prophetic immunity." He reminded Israel of God's help and of their own deviations from God's will, papered over by an empty worship, insufficient to avert inevitable punishment.

One priest, Amaziah, rose to contest Amos and got a particularly scathing retort for his trouble.

Amos reminded his audience that God could and would defend the country against foreign enemies and natural disasters, but only if they left off perverting justice and exploiting the disfranchised among them.

If his countrymen did not establish מִשְׁפָּט (*mispat,* "justice") there would be מִסְפֵּד (*misped,* "lamentation," 5:16-18); God would turn Israel's noon to darkness, overthrow the house of Jeroboam, and turn his countenance with favor upon Judah. This was treason of the worst sort. Better one should be the agent of some foreign government than speak comforting words about the Southern Kingdom.

Sometime after he finished speaking, perhaps immediately following his twenty-minute harangue, Amos left for exile in the South, settling in Tekoa.

Within as few as two years, what Amos said would happen, did happen. Jeroboam died, his heir was murdered and his throne usurped. Members of Amos's "guild," the נֹקְדִים, fled south as rumors circulated that they were involved in the overthrow. Some of them settled in Tekoa, forming a little colony of exiles.

Time passed. A few years later, Assyria began another westward march, the most vigorous and successful yet undertaken. Assyrian armies would overrun Israel and lay siege to Jerusalem before miraculously being pulled back. We do not know how much of this Amos lived to see. But during the remainder of his life he spent some time writing down, to the best of his recollection, the words he had felt compelled to utter. Some few copies circulated among the friends.

When Israel fell, and Judah narrowly escaped the same fate, Amos's friends concluded that he had indeed been commissioned by God to warn the Northern Kingdom. The circle of disciples widened so that, when Judah at length went into exile, there were those in Babylon who knew Amos's words, in their own Northern dialect, by heart.

They brought these words to the attention of Judeans who were gathering the fragments of Israel's prophetic heritage, saving it up in hopes their grandchildren would escape the fate that had overtaken their grandparents.

By the time this happened, no one was quite sure where Amos came from or whether he or Hosea had come first. But that did not matter. The words of Amos were included in the canon.

Though Amos lived more than 2,700 years ago, his words have a disturbingly familiar ring: judges convicted for bribery, government officials misappropriating funds and subverting the laws, whole classes of underprivileged people exploited by those in power. . . . In what age has this not been true? But there is another, more hopeful similarity between Amos's age and ours.

Increasing disparity between rich and poor inevitably creates a "conscience gap," if I may coin a phrase, in which those people who are truly anguished over what they see, even if they are beneficiaries of the system, raise voices of protest. If they are outsiders, we call these people social critics; if insiders, "whistleblowers." My Amos was the latter, an Israelite government functionary who recognized his society's terminal illness and blew such a shrill blast that it echoes in our time.

Earlier generations of Bible readers would have called Amos's motivating force "divine inspiration." In our age of secularism we assume it was Amos's own sensibility at work, so that we can hold out hope for effective social protest even now. In either case, the Amos text we all love seems to be the remarkable record of a single Israelite operating under an inspiring moral compulsion to speak even at his own peril. As he ruefully admits in 5:13, someone with his own self-interest at heart would remain silent, would not want to get involved.

Amos is a hero in the Jewish and Christian traditions because he did not heed his own advice, but risked death and suffered banishment because he could not keep silent. We return to his words again and again for their message of compassion and justice for all.

I hope that when Amos sought refuge in Judean Tekoa many admirers came to visit, and to learn from him.

Bibliography

Ackroyd, Peter R. "Amos vii.14." *Expository Times* 68 (1956/1957): 94.

Aharoni, Yohanan. *The Land of the Bible*. Philadelphia: Westminster Press, 1967.

_____. *See also* Yadin, Yigael.

Aharoni, Yohanan, and Michael Avi-Yonah. *Macmillan Bible Atlas*. Second edition. New York: Macmillan Company, 1977.

Albright, William Foxwell. "Recent Progress in North Canaanite Research." *Bulletin of the American Schools of Oriental Research* no. 70 (April 1936): 18-24.

_____. *Yahweh and the Gods of Canaan*. Garden City NY: Doubleday & Company/Anchor Books, 1969.

Alt, Albrecht. *Essays on Old Testament History and Religion*. Garden City NY: Doubleday & Company/Anchor Books, 1968.

Alter, Robert. *The Art of Biblical Poetry*. New York: Basic Books, 1985.

Amiran, Ruth. *See* Yadin, Yigael.

Andersen, Francis I., and David Noel Freedman. *Hosea. A New Translation with Introduction and Commentary*. Anchor Bible 24. Garden City NY: Doubleday & Company, 1980.

Andersen, Francis I. *See also* Freedman, David Noel.

Anderson, Bernhard. *Understanding the Old Testament*. Englewood Cliffs NJ: Prentice-Hall Inc., 1987.

Arieti, James A. "The Vocabulary of Septuagint Amos." *Journal of Biblical Literature* 93 (1974): 338-47.

Astour, Michael C. "841 B.C.: The First Assyrian Invasion of Israel." *Journal of the American Oriental Society* 91 (1971): 383-89.

Augustine. "De Doctrina Christiana" ("Christian Instruction"). *The Fathers of the Church*. Volume 4. New York: Cima, 1947.

Avi-Yonah, Michael. *See* Aharoni, Yohanan.

Bammel, Ernst. *See* Hauck, Friedrich.

Barstad, Hans M. *The Religious Polemics of Amos. Vetus Testamentum*, supplement 34. Leiden: E. J. Brill, 1984.

Barton, James. *Amos's Oracles against the Nations*. London: Cambridge University Press, 1980.

Beek, Martinus Adrianus. "The Religious Background of Amos 2:6-8." Oudtestamentische Studien 5 (1948): 132-41.

Beeston, Alfred Felix Landon. "Hebrew *šibbolet* and *sobel*." *Journal of Semitic Studies* 24 (1979): 175-77.

Ben-Hayyim, Zeev. *'Ivrit v'aramit nušaḥ šomron* [*The Literary and Oral Tradition of Hebrew and Aramaic amongst the Samaritans*]. Volume 4. Jerusalem: Musad Bialik, Academy of Hebrew Language, 1977.

Ben-Sasson, Haim Hillel, editor. *A History of the Jewish People*. London: George Weidenfeld and Nicholson Ltd., 1969. ET: Cambridge MA: Harvard University Press, 1976.

Bentzen, Aage. *Introduction to the Old Testament*. Copenhagen: Gad, 1961.

Bič, Miloš. "Der Prophet Amos—ein Haepatoskopos." *Vetus Testamentum* 1 (1951): 293-96.

Blau, Joshua. "The Historical Periods of the Hebrew Language." In *Jewish Languages. Themes and Variations*. Edited by Herbert H. Paper. Cambridge MA: Association for Jewish Studies, 1978.

_____. "On Pseudo-Corrections in Some Semitic Languages." *Israel Academic Journal of Sociology and History* (1970). Jerusalem: Israel Academy of Sciences and Humanities, 1970.

_____. " 'Weak' Phonetic Change and the Hebrew SIN." *Hebrew Annual Review* (1977): 67-120.

Blenkinsopp, Joseph A. *A History of Prophecy in Israel*. Philadelphia: Westminster Press, 1983.

Botterweck, G. Johannes. "Zur Authentizität des Buches Amos." *Zeitschrift für die alttestamentische Wissenschaft* 70 (1958): 176-89.

Bright, John. Review of *Joel and Amos* by Hans Walter Wolff. *Interpretation* 25 (1971): 35-56.

Buber, Martin. *The Prophetic Faith*. New York: Harper & Row, 1949.

Brueggemann, Walter. "Amos's Intercessory Formula." *Vetus Testamentum* 19 (1969): 385-99.

Brunet, Gilbert. "La Vision de l'étain: reinterpretation d'Amos 7:7-9." *Vetus Testamentum* 16 (1966): 387-95.

Budde, Karl. "Die Überschrift des Buches Amos und des Propheten Heimat." In *Semitic Studies in Memory of Rev. Dr. Alexander Kohut*, 106-10. Berlin: Calvary, 1897.

_____. "Zu Text und Auslesung des Buches Amos." *Journal of Biblical Literature* 44 (1925): 63-122.

Buss, Martin, editor. *Encounter with the Text*. Philadelphia: Fortress Press, 1979.

Calvin, John (Jean Chauvin). *Commentaries. Minor Prophets*. Jerusalem: Magnes Press, 1950.

Cassuto, Umberto [Moshe David]. *A Commentary on the Book of Genesis*. Two volumes. Translated by Israel Abrahams. Jerusalem: Magnes Press, 1961, 1964.

_____. *The Documentary Hypothesis and the Composition of the Pentateuch*. Jerusalem: Magnes Press, ³1959, 1961.

Chapin, W. *See* Day, Edward.

Childs, Brevard S. *Introduction to the Old Testament as Scripture*. Philadelphia: Fortress Press, 1979.

Christensen, Duane L. *Transformations of the War Oracle in Old Testament Prophecy*. Harvard Dissertations in Religion 3. Missoula MT: Scholars Press, 1975. Especially 57-72.

Clements, Ronald E. *Prophecy and Covenant*. Studies in Biblical Theology 43. London: SCM Press; Naperville IL: Alec R. Allenson Inc., 1965.

Cogan, Morton. *Imperialism and Religion. Assyria, Judah, and Israel in the Eighth and Seventh Centuries B.C.E.* Society of Biblical Literature Monograph Series 19. Missoula MT: Society of Biblical Literature, 1974.

_____. " 'Ripping Open Pregnant Women' in Light of an Assyrian Analogue." *Journal of the American Oriental Society* 103/104 (1983): 755-77.

Cohen, Simon. "Amos *was* a Navi." *Hebrew Union College Annual* 36 (1965): 153-60.

Condamin, Albert. "Amos 1,2–3,8. Authenticité et Structure Poetique." *Revue biblique* 37 (1930): 298-311.

Coote, Robert B. *Amos among the Prophets*. Philadelphia: Fortress Press, 1981.

_____. "Amos 1:11 RHMYW." *Journal of Biblical Literature* 90 (1971): 206-208.

Cornhill, Karl Heinrich. *The Prophets of Israel*. Chicago: Open Court, 1897.

Craghan, John F. "The Prophet Amos in Recent Literature" ["Amos dans la nouvelle recherche"]. *Biblical Theology Bulletin* 2 (1972): 243-62.

Craigie, Peter C. "Amos the נֹקֵד in the Light of Ugaritic." *Studies in Religion/ Sciences religieuses* 11 (1982): 29-33.

Crenshaw, James L. "Amos and the Theophanic Tradition." *Zeitschrift für die alttestamentische Wissenschaft* 80 (1968): 203-15.

_____. *Hymnic Affirmation of Divine Justice. The Doxologies of Amos and Related Texts in the Old Tesatment*. Missoula MT: Scholars Press, 1975.

_____. "The Influence of the Wise on Amos." *Zeitschrift für die alttestamentische Wissenschaft* 79 (1967): 42-52.

_____. *Prophetic Conflict*. Beihefte zu *Zeitschrift für die alttestamentlische Wissenschaft* 124. Berlin: de Gruyter, 1971.

_____. "*Wedôrék algámotê 'āreṣ*." *Catholic Biblical Quarterly* 34 (1972): 39-53.

Cripps, Richard S. *A Critical and Exegetical Commentary on the Book of Amos*. Revised edition. London: S.P.C.K., 1955, = 1960, 1969; ¹1929.

Crowfoot, John, et al. *The Buildings of Samaria*. Second edition. London: Palestine Exploration Fund, 1966.

Dahood, Mitchell J. "Amos 6:8 *metā' ēb*." *Biblica* 59 (1978): 265-66.

_____. "Can One Plow without Oxen?" In *The Bible World. Essays in Honor of Cyrus H. Gordon*, edited by Gary Rendsburg, 13-23. New York: KTAV Publishing House, 1981.

Dalman, Gustaf. *Orte und Weg Jesu*. Gütersloh: Bertelsmann, 1924.

Davila, James R. "Qoheleth and Northern Hebrew." Manuscript copy of Davila's paper "Qoheleth and Northern Hebrew," presented to the SBL Northwest Semitic Epigraphy Group at the AAR/SBL annual meeting in Atlanta, November 1986, and to be published in the Segert Festschrift, forthcoming.

Davis, John J. *Biblical Numerology*. Grand Rapids MI; Baker Book House, 1968.

Davies, Gwynne Henton. "Amos—the Prophet of Re-Union." *Expository Times* 92/7 (1981): 196-200.

Day, Edward, and W. Chapin. "Is the Book of Amos Post-Exilic?" *American Journal of Semitic Languages and Literatures* 18 (1901/1902): 65-93.

de Vaux, Roland. *Ancient Israel. Its Life and Institutions*. London: Darton, Longman & Todd; New York: McGraw-Hill Book Company, 1961; McGraw-Hill two-volume paperback edition, 1965.

Dijkema, F. "Le fond des prophéties d'Amos." Oudtestamentische Studien 2 (1943): 18-34.

Dobbie, Robert. "Amos 5:25." *Transactions of the Glasgow University Oriental Society* 17 (1959): 62-64.

Donner, Herbert. "The Separate States of Israel and Judah." In Hayes and Miller, *History* (below), 381-434.

Dothan, Trude. *See* Yadin, Yigael.

Driver, Godfrey Rolles. "A Hebrew Burial Custom." *Zeitschrift für die alttestamentliche Wissenschaft* 66 (1954): 314-15.

_____. "Two Astronomical Passages in the Old Testament." *Journal of Theological Studies* n.s. 4 (1953): 208-12.

Driver, Samuel Rolles, with H. C. O. Lanchester. *The Books of Joel and Amos*. The Cambridge Bible for Schools and Colleges. Second edition. Cambridge: Cambridge University Press, 1915; ¹1897.

Dunayevsky, Emmanuel. *See* Yadin, Yigael.

Dupont-Sommer, André. *Les Araméens*. L'Orient Ancien Illustré 2. Paris: A. Maisonneuve, 1949.

Efrat, Elisha. *See* Orni, Ephraim.

Ehrlich, Arnold B. *Mikra k'peshuto* [Hebrew]. New York: KTAV Publishing House, 1969; ¹1898.

Eitan, Israel. "Biblical Studies." *Hebrew Union College Annual* 14 (1939): 1-22 (only page 6).

Eissfeldt, Otto. *The Old Testament. An Introduction*. Translated by P. R. Ackroyd. Oxford: Basil Blackwell; New York: Harper & Row, 1965.

Even-Shoshan, Abraham. *A Concordance of the Old Testament*. Jerusalem: Kiryat Sepher Publishing House, 1983.

Farr, Georges. "The Language of Amos: Popular or Cultic?" *Vetus Testamentum* 16 (1966): 317-24.

Feldman, W. M. *Rabbinic Mathematics and Astronomy*. Third edition. New York: Hermon Press, 1978; ¹1931.

Feliks, Jehuda. *The Animal World of the Bible*. Tel Aviv: Sinai, 1962.

Fishbane, Michael. *Biblical Interpretation in Ancient Israel*. London: Oxford University Press, 1985.

_____. "The Treaty Background of Amos 1:11 and Related Matters." *Journal of Biblical Literature* 89 (1970): 313-18.

Fohrer, Georg. *Introduction to the Old Testament*. Translated by D. E. Green. Nashville: Abingdon Press, 1968; London, 1970.

_____. "Remarks on Modern Interpretation of the Prophets." *Journal of Biblical Literature* 80 (1961): 309-19.

_____. "Zion-Jerusalem in the Old Testament" [Part A of the article on Σιών]. In volume 7 of *Theological Dictionary of the New Testament,* edited by Gerhard Friedrich, translated and edited by Geoffrey W. Bromiley, 293-327. Grand Rapids MI: Eerdmans, 1971.

Frankfort, Henri. *Kingship and the Gods*. Chicago: University of Chicago Press, 1948.

Freedman, David Noel. "Archaeology and the Future of Biblical Studies." In *The Bible and Modern Scholarship,* edited by J. Philip Hyatt, 294-312. Nashville: Abingdon Press, 1965.

Freedman, David Noel. *See also* Andersen, Francis I.

Freedman, David Noel, and Francis I. Andersen. "Harmon in Amos 4:3." *Bulletin of the American Schools of Oriental Research* no. 198 (1970): 41.

Frye, Northrop. *The Great Code. The Bible and Literature*. New York: Harcourt, Brace, Jovanovich, 1965.

Gamberoni, J. בָּרַח. In volume 2 of *Theological Dictionary of the Old Testament,* revised edition, edited by G. Johannes Botterweck and Helmer Ringgren, translated by John T. Willis, 249-53. Grand Rapids MI: Eerdmans, 1977; ¹1975.

Gardiner, Alan. *See* Langdon, Stephen.

Garr, W. Randall. *Dialect Geography of Syria-Palestine, 1000–586 BCE.* Philadelphia: University of Pennsylvania Press, 1985.

Gaster, Theodor Herzl. *Thespis.* New York: Harper & Row, 1961.

Gerstenberger, Erhard. "Covenant and Commandment." *Journal of Biblical Literature* 84 (1965): 38-51.

_____. "The Woe Oracles of the Prophets." *Journal of Biblical Literature* 81 (1962): 249-63.

Gevirtz, Stanley. "A New Look at an Old Crux, Amos 5:26." *Journal of Biblical Literature* 87 (1968): 267-76.

Gilead, Chaim. "Amos—from the Herdsmen in Tekoa." *Beth Mikra* 54 (1973): 375-81.

Ginsberg, Harold Louis. *The Book of Isaiah.* Philadelphia: Jewish Publication Society, 1973.

_____. *The Israelian Heritage of Judaism.* New York: Jewish Theological Seminary, 1982.

_____. " 'Roots Below and Fruits Above' and Related Matters." In *Hebrew and Semitic Studies Presented to G. R. Driver,* edited by D. Winton Thomas and W. D. McHardy, 59-71. London: Oxford University Press, 1963.

Gitay, Yehoshua. "A Study of Amos's Art of Speech. A Rhetorical Analysis of Amos 3:1-15." *Catholic Biblical Quarterly* 42 (1980): 293-309.

Goodman, Nelson. "On Likeness of Meaning." In *Philosophy and Analysis,* ed. M. Macdonald, 54-62. New York: Philosophical Library, 1954.

Gordis, Robert. "The Composition and Structure of Amos." *Harvard Theological Review* 33 (1940): 239-51.

_____. "Quotations as a Literary Usage in Biblical, Rabbinic, and Oriental Literature." *Hebrew Union College Annual* 22 (1949): 157-220.

_____. "The Heptad as an Element in Biblical and Rabbinic Style." *Journal of Biblical Literature* 62 (1943): 17-26.

Gordon, Cyrus Herzl. *Ugarit and Minoan Crete.* New York: W. W. Norton, 1966.

Gottwald, Norman Karol. "Sociological Method in the Study of Ancient Israel." In Buss, *Encounter with the Text,* above.

_____. *The Tribes of Yahweh.* Maryknoll: Orbis, 1979.

Gray, John. *1 and 2 Kings. A Commentary.* Old Testament Library. Philadelphia: Westminster Press, 1963.

Greenfield, Jonas C. "Aramaic and Its Dialects." In H. Paper, *Jewish Languages,* below.

_____. "Dialect Traits in Early Aramaic." *Lešonénu* 32 (1960): 359-68.

_____. "The MARZEAH as a Social Institution." In *Wirtschaft und Gesellschaft im alten Vorderasien,* edited by Joseph Harmatta, 451-55. Budapest: Akademiai Kiodo, 1974–1976.

Gross, Nachum, editor. *Economic History of the Jews.* New York: Schocken, 1975.

Grossfeld, Bernard. "The Relationship between Biblical Hebrew ברח and נוס and Their Corresponding Aramaic Equivalents in the Targum—ערק, ספר, אזל: A Preliminary Study in Hebrew Lexicography." *Zeitschrift für die alttestamentlische Wissenschaft* 91 (1979): 107-23.

Hallo, William W. "From Qarqar to Carchemish: Assyria and Israel in the Light of New Discoveries." *The Biblical Archaeologist* 23 (1960): 34-61.

Hammerschaimb, Erling. *The Book of Amos. A Commentary.* Translated by John Sturdy. Oxford: Basil Blackwell; New York: Schocken, 1970. Original: *Amos Fortolket.* Kjøbenhavn: Nyt NOrdisk, 1946, ²1958, ³1967.

Haran, Menahem. "Amos." *Encyclopedia Judaica.* Jerusalem: Keter, 1971. (Haran's own translation of his article in *Encyclopedia Miqrait.*)

_____. "Observations on the Historical Background of Amos 1:2–2:6." *Israel Exploration Journal* 18 (1968): 201-12.

_____. "The Rise and Decline of the Empire of Jeroboam ben Joash." *Vetus Testamentum* 17 (1967): 272-78.

Harper, William Rainey. *A Critical and Exegetical Commentary on Amos and Hosea.* International Critical Commentary. Edinburgh: T. & T. Clark, 1905.

Harris, Zellig Sabettai. *Development of the Canaanite Dialects.* American Oriental Series 8. New Haven CT: Yale University Press, 1939.

_____. *A Grammar of the Phoenician Language.* Philadelphia: Jewish Publication Society, 1936.

Hauck, Friedrich, and Ernst Bammel. πτωχός κτλ. In volume 6 of *Theological Dictionary of the New Testament,* edited by Gerhard Friedrich, translated and edited by Geoffrey W. Bromiley, 885-915. Grand Rapids MI: Eerdmans, 1968.

Hayes, John H. "The Usage of Oracles against Foreign Nations in Ancient Israel." *Journal of Biblical Literature* 87 (1968): 81-92.

_____. *Amos: The Eighth-Century Prophet. His Times and His Preaching.* Nashville: Abingdon, 1988.

Hayes, John H., and J. Maxwell Miller, editors. *Israelite and Judean History.* Old Testament Library. Philadelphia: Westminster Press; London: SCM Press, 1977.

Herrmann, Siegfried. *A History of Israel in Old Testament Times*. Philadelphia: Fortress Press, 1975.

Heschel, Abraham Joshua. *The Prophets*. New York: Harper & Row, 1962.

Hoffmann, Hans Werner. "Zur Echtheitfrage von Amos 9:9f." *Zeitschrift für die alttestamentliche Wissenschaft* 82 (1970): 121-22.

Hoffman, Yair. "Did Amos Regard Himself as a NABI?" *Vetus Testamentum* 27 (1977): 209-12.

Hogg, Hope W. "The Starting Point of the Religious Message of Amos." *Transactions of the Third Congress for the History of Religions*, 1:325-27. Edited by P. S. Allen and J. deM. Johnson. Oxford, 1908.

Holladay, William L. "Amos 6:16b. A Suggested Solution." *Vetus Testamentum* 22 (1972): 107-10.

_____. "Once More 'Anak = Tin, Amos 7:7f." *Vetus Testamentum* 20 (1970): 492-94.

Hoonacker, Albin van. "Notes d'exegèse sur quelques passages difficiles d'Amos." *Revue biblique* 14 (1905): 163-87.

Hyatt, J. Philip. *The Bible in Modern Scholarship*. Nashville: Abingdon Press, 1965.

_____. "The Translation and Meaning of Amos 5:23-24." *Zeitschrift für die alttestamentliche Wissenschaft* 68 (1956): 17-24.

Irwin, William A. "The Thinking of Amos." *American Journal of Semitic Languages and Literatures* 49 (1933); 102-14.

Isbell, Charles. "A Note on Amos 1:1." *Journal of Near Eastern Studies* 36 (1977): 213-15.

Jacobson, Thorkild. *The Treasures of Darkness*. New Haven CT: Yale University Press, 1976.

Jastrow, Morris. *A Dictionary of the Targumim, the Talmud Babli and Yerushalmi, and the Midrashic Literature*. New York: Pardes, 1950.

Johnson, Aubrey R. *The Cultic Prophet in Ancient Israel*. Second edition. Cardiff: University of Wales Press, 1962; ¹1944.

Jongeling, B. "La particule רק." Oudtestamentische Studien 18 (1973): 97-107.

Joüon, Paul. "Notes de critique textuelle." *Mélanges de l'université de Saint-Joseph* 4 (1910): 30.

Jozaki, Susamu. "The Secondary Passages of the Book of Amos." *Kwansei University Annual Studies* 4 (1956): 25-100.

Kahan, Arcadius. "Viticulture." *Encyclopedia Judaica* 16:1268.

Kapelrud, Arvid Schou. *Central Ideas in Amos*. Oslo: Oslo University Press, 1961.

_____. "God as Destroyer in the Preaching of Amos." *Journal of Biblical Literature* 71 (1952): 33-38.

_____. "New Ideas in Amos." *Vetus Testamentum,* Supplement 15 (1965): 193-206.

Kassis, Hanna E. "Gath and Philistine Society." *Journal of Biblical Literature* 84 (1965): 259-71.

Kaufmann, Yehezkel. *The Religion of Israel. From Its Beginnings to the Babylonian Exile.* Translated by Moshe Greenberg. Chicago: University of Chicago Press, 1960; New York: Schocken, 1972. (This is the translation of an abridgement of the first six volumes [in Hebrew] of Kaufmann's major work.)

_____. *Toledot HaEmunah HaYisraelit.* Four volumes. Tel Aviv: Mujsad Bialik, 1937–1956.

Kellermann, Ulrich. "Der Amosschluss als Stimme Deuteronomistichen Heilshoffnung." *Evangelische Theologie* 29 (1969): 169-83.

Kelly, John Norman David. *Jerome. His Life, Writings, and Controversies.* New York: Harper & Row, 1975.

Kenyon, Kathleen Mary. *The Bible and Recent Archaeology.* Atlanta: John Knox Press, 1978.

_____. *Royal Cities of the Old Testament.* New York: Schocken, 1971.

King, Philip J. *Amos, Hosea, Micah—An Archaeological Commentary.* Philadelphia: Westminster, 1988.

Knierim, Rolf. " 'I will not cause it to return' in Amos 1 and 2." In *Canon and Authority* (W. Zimmerli Festschrift), edited by G. Coats, 163-75. Philadelphia: Fortress Press, 1977.

_____. "Old Testament Criticism Reconsidered." *Interpretation* 27 (1973): 435-68.

Kraabel, James. *See* Meyer, Eric.

Kraeling, Emil. *The Prophets.* Chicago: Rand McNally, 1956.

Krause, Hans Helmut. "Die Gerichtsprophet Amos, ein Vorlaufer des Deuteronomisten." *Zeitschrift für die alttestamentlische Wissenschaft* 50 (1932): 221-39.

Kugel, James. *The Ideas of Biblical Poetry.* New Haven CT: Yale University Press, 1981.

Kutscher, Eduard Yechezkel. *A History of the Hebrew Language.* Edited by Raphael Kutscher. Jerusalem: Magnes Press; Leiden: E. J. Brill, 1982.

Laessøe, Jorgen. "The Building Inscription at Fort Shalmaneser, Nimrud." *Iraq* 21 (1959): 38-41.

Landsberger, Benno. "Tin and Lead—the Adventures of Two Vocables." *Journal of Near Eastern Studies* 24 (1965): 285-96.

Lang, Bernhard. "The Social Organization of Peasant Poverty in Biblical Israel." *Journal for the Study of the Old Testament* 24 (1982): 47-63.

_____. "Sklaven und Unfreie im Buch Amos (2:6–8:6)." *Vetus Testamentum* 31 (1981): 482-88.

Langdon, Stephen, and Alan Gardiner. "The Treaty of Alliance between Hattusili, King of the Hittites, and the Pharaoh Ramses II of Egypt." *Journal of Egyptology and Assyriology* 6 (1923): 179-205.

Lehming, Sigo. "Erwagungen zu Amos." *Zeitschrift für Theologie und Kirche* 55 (1958): 145-69.

Leiman, Schnayer Z. (Sid). *The Canon and Masorah of the Hebrew Bible.* New York: Arno Press, 1974.

Limburg, James. "Amos 7:14. A Judgement with Fire." *Catholic Biblical Quarterly* 35 (1973): 346-49.

Lindblom, Johannes. *Prophecy in Ancient Israel.* Philadelphia: Fortress Press, 1962, ²1963. Original: *Profetismen in Israel.* 1934.

Loewenstamm, Samuel E. "The Address 'Listen' in the Ugaritic Epic and the Bible." In *The Bible World,* edited by Gary A. Rendsburg, 123-31. New York: KTAV Publishing House, 1981.

Luria, Ben Zion. "Amos—Prophet and Worldly Man." *Dor le Dor* 10 (1982): 183-86.

Lust, J. "Remarks on the Redaction of Amos 5:4-6, 14-15." Oudtestamentische Studien 21 (1981): 129-55.

Maag, Victor. *Text, Wortschatz, und Begriffswelt des Buches Amos.* Leiden: E. J. Brill, 1951.

Malamat, Abraham. "Amos 1:5 in the Light of the Til Barsip Inscriptions." *Bulletin of the American Schools of Oriental Research* no. 129 (1953): 25-26.

_____. "Prophetic Revelations in New Documents from Mari and the Bible." *Vetus Testamentum* 15 (1965): 207-28.

_____. *Sources for Early Biblical History.* Jerusalem: Academon Press, 1970.

Mandelkern, Solomon. *Lexicon in Veteris Testamentii Hebraicae atque Chaldaicae.* Fourth edition. Tel Aviv: Schocken Publishing House Ltd., 1962; ¹1896.

Mays, James Luther. *Amos. A Commentary.* Old Testament Library. Philadelphia: Westminster Press, 1969.

McKeating, Henry. *The Books of Amos, Hosea, and Micah.* The Cambridge Bible Commentary on the New English Bible. Cambridge: Cambridge University Press, 1971.

Martin-Achard, Robert, and S. Paul Re'emi. *Amos and Lamentations. God's People in Crisis.* International Theological Commentary. Grand Rapids MI: Eerdmans, 1984.

Mazar, Benjamin. "Gath and Gittaim." *Israel Exploration Journal* 4 (1954): 227-35.

Meek, Theophile J. "Again the Accusative of Time in Amos 1:1." *Journal of the American Oriental Society* 61 (1941): 190-91.

_____. "The Accusative of Time in Amos 1:1." *Journal of the American Oriental Society* 61 (1941): 63-64.

Melamed, Ezra Zion. "Breakup of Stereotype Phrases as an Artistic Device in Hebrew Poetry." *Scripta Hierosolymitana* 8 (1961): 115-44.

Meyer, Eric, James Kraabel, and James Strange. *Ancient Synagogue Excavations at Khirbet Shema.* Annual of the American Schools of Oriental Research 42. Durham NC: Duke University Press, 1977.

Miller, J. Maxwell. *See* Hayes, John H.

Miller, Patrick. "God the Warrior." *Interpretation* 19 (1965): 45.

Mittmann, Siegfried. "Amos 3:12-15 und das Bett der Samarier." *Zeitschrift für des Deutschen Palastina-Vereins* 92 (1976): 149-67.

Montgomery, James A. "Notes from the Samaritan (2) the Root פרט, Amos 6:5." *Journal of Biblical Literature* 25 (1906): 51-52.

_____. "Notes on the Old Testament." *Journal of Biblical Literature* 31 (1912): 140-46.

Moortgat, Anton. *The Art of Ancient Mesopotamia.* London: Phaidon Press, 1969.

Morgenstern, Julian. "The Address of Amos— Text and Commentary." *Hebrew Union College Annual* 32 (1961): 295-350.

_____. "Amos Studies I." *Hebrew Union College Annual* 11 (1936): 19-140; "Amos Studies II," HUCA 12-13 (1937-1938): 1-53; "Amos Studies III," HUCA 15 (1940): 59-304; "Amos Studies IV," HUCA 32 (1961): 295-350. Morgenstern's "Amos Studies I, II, and III" were reprinted as *Amos Studies.* Volume 1. Cincinnati: Hebrew Union College, 1941.

_____. "Jerusalem—485 B.C.E." *Hebrew Union College Annual* 27 (1956): 101-80; 28 (1957): 15-48; 31 (1960): 1-30.

_____. "The Loss of Words at the Ends of Lines in Biblical Poetry." *Hebrew Union College Annual* 25 (1954): 41-83.

Moscati, Sabatino. *An Introduction to the Comparative Grammar of the Semitic Languages.* Wiesbaden: Otto Harrassowitz, 1964.

Muilenburg, James. "The Office of Prophet in Ancient Israel." In Hyatt, *The Bible in Modern Scholarship,* above, 74-97.

Munch, Peter Andreas. "Einige Bemerkungen zu den עֲנָוִים und den רְשָׁעִים in den Psalmen." *Le Monde Orientale* 30 (1936): 13-14.

Murtonen, André E. "Amos—ein Haepatoscopos?" *Vetus Testamentum* 2 (1952): 170-71.

Na'aman, Nadav. "Royal Estates in the Jezreel Valley in the Late Bronze Age and Under the Israelite Monarchy." *Eretz Yisrael* 15 (Aharoni Memorial

Volume, 1981): 14-144. Jerusalem: Israel Exploration Society. (Hebrew, with English summary on page 81.)

_____. "Sennacherib's 'Letter to God' on His Campaign to Judah." *Bulletin of the American Oriental Society* 214 (1974): 25-39.

Nagah, Ruth. "Are You Not Like the Ethiopians to Me?" *Beth Miqra* 27 (1981/1982): 174-82.

Neher, André. *Amos. Contribution a l'étude du Prophetisme.* Paris: J. Vrin, 1950.

Neubauer, Karl Wilhelm. "Erwagungen zu Amos 5:4-15." *Zeitschrift für die alttestamentliche Wissenschaft* 78 (1966): 292-316.

Neugebauer, Otto. *The Exact Sciences in Antiquity.* New York: Dover, 1969; ¹1949.

Noth, Martin. *The Wisdom of Israel.* London: Adam and Charles Black, 1960.

Nowack, Wilhelm. *Die Kleine Propheten.* Kommentar zum Alten Testament. Göttingen: Vandenhoeck und Rupprecht, 1903.

Oded, Benjamin. *Mass Deportation and Deportees in the Neo-Assyrian Empire.* Wiesbaden: Reichert, 1976.

Oesterley, W. O. E. *Studies in Greek and Latin Versions of the Book of Amos.* Cambridge: Cambridge University Press, 1902.

Olmstead, Alfred T. *History of Assyria.* Chicago: University of Chicago Press, 1923.

Oppenheim, A. Leo. *Ancient Mesopotamia.* Chicago: University of Chicago Press, 1964.

Orni, Ephraim, and Elisha Efrat. *Geography of Israel.* Third revised edition. Jerusalem: Jewish Theological Seminary, 1973.

Overholt, Thomas. "Commanding the Prophets. Amos and the Problem of Prophetic Authority." *Catholic Biblical Quarterly* 41 (1979): 517-32.

Page, Stephanie, "A Stela of Adad-nirari III and Nergal-eres from Tell al Rumiah." *Iraq* 30 (1968): 139-53.

Paper, Herbert H. *Jewish Languages. Theme and Variations.* Cambridge MA: Association for Jewish Studies, 1978.

Paul, Shalom M. "Amos 1:3–2:3. A Concatenous Literary Pattern." *Journal of Biblical Literature* 90 (1971): 397-403.

_____. "A Literary Reinvestigation of the Authenticity of the Oracles against the Nations of Amos." In *De la Torah au Messie. Études d'exegèse et d'hermeneutique biblique offertes à Henri Cazelles,* edited by Maurice Carrez, Joseph Dore, and Pierre Grelot, 187-204. Paris: Desclée, 1981.

_____. "Amos 3:15— Winter and Summer Mansions." *Vetus Testamentum* 28 (1978): 358-60.

_____. "Fishing Imagery in Amos." *Journal of Biblical Literature* 97 (1978): 183-90.

Perrot, Jean. *See* Yadin, Yigael.

Peters, John Punnett. *The Psalms as Liturgies.* New York: Macmillan Company, 1920.

Pfeiffer, Robert H. "Facts and Faith in Biblical History." *Journal of Biblical Literature* 70 (1971): 1-14.

Piotrovsky, Boris B. *The Ancient Civilization of Urartu.* Translated by James Hogarth. New York: Cowles Book Co., 1969.

Polley, Max E. *Amos and the Davidic Empire.* New York: Oxford University Press, 1989.

Porter, J. Roy. *"Benê hannevi'îm." Journal of Theological Studies* 32 (1981): 423-29.

Praetorius, Franz. "Zum Texte des Amos." *Zeitschrift für die alttestamentliche Wissenschaft* 34 (1914): 42-44.

Pritchard, James. *Ancient Near Eastern Texts Relating to the Old Testament.* Third edition revised. Princeton NJ: Princeton University Press, 1969.

Priest, John. "The Covenant of Brothers." *Journal of Biblical Literature* 84 (1965): 400-406.

Puech, E. "Milkom, le Dieu Ammonite en Amos 1:15." *Vetus Testamentum* 27 (1977): 117-25.

Rabin, Chaim. "BARIAH." *Journal of Theological Studies* 47 (1946): 38-41.

Rabinowitz, Isaac. "The Crux of Amos 3:12." *Vetus Testamentum* 11 (1961): 228-31.

Rahlfs, Alfred. *'ānī und 'ānāw in den Psalmen.* Göttingen: Vandenhoeck und Rupprecht, 1892.

Rainey, Anson F. "The Identification of Philistine Gath. A Problem in Source Analysis for Historical Geography." *Eretz Israel* 12 (Nelson Glueck Memorial Volume; Jerusalem: Israel Exploration Society, 1975): 63-76.

Ramsay, G. W. "Amos 4:12, a New Perspective." *Journal of Biblical Literature* 89 (1970): 187-91.

Re'emi, S. Paul. *See* Martin-Achard, Robert.

Reider, Joseph. "דמשק in Amos 3:12." *Journal of Biblical Literature* 67 (1948): 245-48.

_____. "Index to Aquila." *Vetus Testamentum,* Supplement 12. Leiden: E. J. Brill, 1966.

Rendsburg, Gary A., editor. *The Bible World. Essays in Honor of Cyrus H. Gordon.* New York: KTAV Publishing House, 1981.

_____. "Evidence for a Spoken Hebrew in Biblical Times." Ph.D. dissertation, New York University, 1980; Ann Arbor MI: University Microfilms, 1981.

Reventlow, Henning Graf von. *Das Amt des Propheten bei Amos*. Forschungen zur Religion und Literatur des Alten und Neuen Testaments 80. Göttingen: Vandenhoeck und Rupprecht, 1962.

Richardson, H. Neil. "SKT (Amos 9:11) 'Booth' or 'Succoth'?" *Journal of Biblical Literature* 92 (1973): 375-81.

Robinson, Theodore H. *The Book of Amos. Hebrew Text Edited with Critical and Grammatical Notes*. Texts for Students 30. London: S.P.C.K., 1923, 1951.

Rosenbaum, Stanley Ned. "A Northern Amos Revisited. Two Philological Suggestions." *Hebrew Studies* 15 (1977): 132-48.

Rosenthal, Franz. *A Grammar of Biblical Aramaic*. Wiesbaden: Otto Harrassowitz, 1963.

Roth, Wolfgang M. W. "The Numeral Sequence x/x + 1 in the Old Testament." *Vetus Testamentum* 12 (1962): 300-11.

Rowley, Harold Henry. "Was Amos a *Nabi*?" In *Festschrift für Otto Eissfeldt*, edited by Johann Fück, 191-98. Halle an der Salle: Max Niemeyer, 1947.

Rudolph, Wilhelm. *Joel—Amos—Obadja—Jona*. Kommentar zum Alten Testament 13/2. Edited by Ernst Sellin. Gütersloh: Gütersloher Verlagshaus (Gerd Mohn), 1971.

San Nicolo, Mariano. "Materielen zur Viehwirtschaft in den Neubabylonischen Templen." *Orientalia* new series 17 (1948): 273-93.

Saggs, H. W. F. *The Greatness That Was Babylon*. New York: Signet, 1968, 1962.

Sarna, Nahum M. "The Interchange of the Prepositions *bēt* and *min* in Biblical Hebrew." *Journal of Biblical Literature* 78 (1959): 310-16.

Schmidt, Hans. "Die Herkunft des Propheten Amos." In *Karl Budde zum siebzigsten Geburtstag*, edited by Karl Marti, 158-71. Beihefte zur *Zeitschrift für die alttestamentliche Wissenschaft* 34. Giessen: Topelmann, 1920.

_____. *Der Prophet Amos*. Tübingen: J. C. B. Mohr, 1917.

Schoville, Keith N. "A Note on the Oracles of Amos against Gaza, Tyre, and Edom." *Vetus Testamentum*, Supplement 26 (1974): 55-63.

Schwantes, Siegfried. "Notes on Amos 4:2b." *Zeitschrift für die alttestamentliche Wissenschaft* 79 (1967): 82-83.

Segert, Stanislav. "A Controlling Device for Copying Stereotype Passages? (Amos 1:3–2:8; 6:1-6)." *Vetus Testamentum* 34 (1984): 481-82.

_____. *A Grammar of Phoenician and Punic*. Munich: Beck, 1976.

Sellin, Ernst. *Das Zwölfprophetenbuch übersetzt und erklärt*. Kommentar zum Alten Testament 12. Leipzig: Erlangen, 1922, ²1929, ³1930.

Silver, Morris. *Prophets and Markets. The Political Economy of Ancient Israel*. Boston: Kluwer, 1983.

Smalley, William Allen. "Recursion Patterns and the Sectioning of Amos." *The Bible Translator* 30 (1979): 118-27.

Smith, George Adam. *Amos, Hosea, and Micah.* Volume 1 of *The Book of the Twelve Prophets Commonly Called the Minor.* Two volumes. The Expositor's Bible. London: Hodder & Stoughton; New York: George H. Doran, (1)1896, (2)1898; New York: Harper & Brothers, ²1928.

Smith, W. Robertson. *The Prophets of Israel and Their Place in History.* New York: D. Appleton & Co., 1892.

Snaith, Norman Henry. *Amos, Hosea, and Micah.* Epworth Preacher's Commentaries. London: Epworth Press, 1956.

_____. *The Book of Amos.* Part 1. *Introduction.* Part 2. *Translation and Notes.* Study Notes on Bible Books. London: Epworth Press, (1) 1945, 1957; (2) 1946, 1958.

Soggin, J. Alberto. "Das Erdbeden von Amos 1:1 und die Chronologie der Konige Ussia und Jotham von Juda." *Zeitschrift für die alttestamentliche Wissenschaft* 82 (1970): 116-21.

Sontag, Raymond. *European Diplomatic History, 1871–1932.* New York: Appleton, 1933.

Soper, B. Kingston. "For Three Transgressions and for Four. A New Interpretation of Amos 1:3." *Expository Times* 71 (1959/1960): 86-87.

Speier, Salomon. "Bemerkungen zu Amos." *Vetus Testamentum* 3 (1953): 305-306.

Speiser, Ephraim Avigdon. "A Note on Amos 5:26." *Bulletin of the American Schools of Oriental Research* 108 (1947): 5-6.

_____. "The Pronunciation of Hebrew." *Jewish Quarterly Review* 23 (1933): 233-65.

_____. "The Shibboleth Incident." In *Oriental and Biblical Studies,* edited by Moshe Greenberg and J. J. Finkelstein, 143-50. Philadelphia: University of Pennsylvania Press, 1967.

Sperber, Alexander. *A Historical Grammar of Biblical Hebrew.* Leiden: E. J. Brill, 1966.

Spiegel, Shalom. "Amos vs. Amaziah." In *The Jewish Expression,* edited by Judah Goldin, 38-65. New York: Bantam, 1970; New Haven CT: Yale University Press, 1976.

Spinoza, Baruch (Benedict). *A Theologico-Political Treatise.* Translated by R. H. M. Elwes. New York: Dover Publications, 1951.

Steiner, Richard C. *Affricated Ṣade in the Semitic Languages.* New York: American Academy for Jewish Research, 1982.

Steinkeller, Piotr. "The Old Akkadian Term for [Easterner]." *Revue d'assyriologie et d'archaeologie orientale* 74 (1980): 1-9 (only page 9).

Stoebe, Hans-Joachim. "Der Prophet Amos und sein burgerlicher Beru." *Wort und Dienst* 5 (1957): 160-81.

Story, Cullen. "Amos—Prophet of Praise." *Vetus Testamentum* 30 (1980): 67-80.

Strange, James. *See* Meyer, Eric.

Szabo, A. "Textual Problems in Amos and Hosea." *Vetus Testamentum* 25 (1975): 500-508.

Tadmor, Ḥaim. "Azriyau of Yaudi." *Scripta Hierosolymitana* 8 (1961): 232-71.

_____. "The Historical Background of Hosea's Prophecies" [Hebrew]. In *Yehezkel Kaufmann Jubilee Volume,* edited by Menahem Haran, 74-78. Jerusalem: Magnes Press, 1960.

Talmon, Shemaryahu. "Double Reading in the Masoretic Text." *Textus* 1 (1960): 144-84.

_____. "The Gezer Calendar and the Seasonal Cycle of Ancient Canaan." *Journal of the American Oriental Society* 83 (1963): 177-87.

Terrien, Samuel. "Amos and Wisdom." In *Israel's Prophetic Heritage,* edited by Bernhard W. Anderson and Walter Harrelson, 108-15. New York: Harper, 1962.

Thiele, Edwin R. *A Chronology of the Hebrew Kings.* Grand Rapids MI: Zondervan, 1983. (Revised and updated edition of his *The Mysterious Numbers of the Hebrew Kings.* Third edition. Chicago: University of Chicago Press, 1963.)

Thomas, David Winton. *Documents from Old Testament Times.* New York: Harper, 1958.

_____. "Note on נוֹעָדוּ in Amos 3:3." *Journal of Theological Studies* new series 7 (1956): 69-70.

Torczyner, Naphtali Herz (Harry). [*See also* N. H. Tur-Sinai.] "Presidential Address." *Journal of the Palestine Oriental Society* 16 (1936): 1-8.

Toy, Crawford Howell. "The Judgement of Foreign Peoples in Amos 1:3–2:3." *Journal of Biblical Literature* 25 (1906): 25-28.

Tucker, Gene. "Prophetic Authenticity. A Form-Critical Study of Amos 7:10-17." *Interpretation* 27 (1973): 423-34.

Tur-Sinai, Naphtali Herz. [*See also* Torczyner.] *Job. A New Commentary.* Jerusalem: Kiriath-Sepher, 1957.

Ullmann, Steven. *The Principles of Semantics.* London: Oxford University Press, 1963.

Van Leeuwen, Raymond C. "The Prophecy of the *Yōm YHVH* in Amos 5:18-20." In *Language and Meaning: Studies in Hebrew Language and Biblical Exegesis,* Oudtestamentische Studien 19, 113-34. Leiden: E. J. Brill, 1974.

Vesco, Jean-Luc. "Amos de Teqoa, Défenseur de l'Homme." *Revue Biblique* 87 (1980): 481-513.

Vuilleumier-Bessard, René. *La tradition cultuelle d'Israël dans la prophétie d'Amos et d'Osée,* 88-90. Cahiers Théologiques 45. Neuchâtel and Paris: Delachaux et Niestle, 1960.

Wagner, Siegfried. "Überlegungen zur Frage nach Bezehungen des Propheten Amos zum Sudreich." *Theologische Literarzeitung* 96 (Leipzig, 1971): 653-70.

Wanke, Gunther. "אוי und הוי." *Zeitschrift für die alttestamentliche Wissenschaft* 78 (1966): 215-18.

Watts, John D. W. "An Old Hymn Preserved in the Book of Amos." *Journal of Near Eastern Studies* 15 (1956): 33-39.

_____. "The Origin of the Book of Amos." *Expository Times* 66 (1954/ 1955): 109-12.

_____. *Vision and Prophecy in Amos*. Grand Rapids MI: Eerdmans, 1958.

Weiser, Artur. *Die Prophetie von Amos*. Beihefte zur *Zeitschrift für die alttestamentliche Wissenschaft* 53. Giessen: Topelmann, 1929.

_____. *The Old Testament. Its Formation and Development*. Translated by D. M. Barton. London; New York: Association Press, 1961.

Weiss, Meir. "The Pattern of Numerical Sequence in Amos 1–2." *Journal of Biblical Literature* 86 (1967): 416-23.

Westermann, Claus. *Basic Forms of Prophetic Speech*. Philadelphia: Westminster Press, 1967.

Williams, A. J. "Further Suggestions about Amos 4:1-3." *Vetus Testamentum* 29 (1979): 206-11.

Willis, John. "Redaction Criticism and Historical Reconstruction." In *Encounter with the Text,* edited by Martin Buss. Philadelphia: Fortress Press, 1979.

Wilson, Robert R. *Prophecy and Society in Ancient Israel*. Philadelphia: Fortress Press, 1980. Especially pages 266-70.

Wolff, Hans Walter. *Amos the Prophet. The Man and His Background*. Translated by Foster R. McCurley. Philadelphia: Fortress Press, 1973.

_____. *Joel and Amos. A Commentary on the Books of the Prophets Joel and Amos*. Translated by Waldemar Janzen, S. Dean McBride, Jr., and Charles A Muenchow. Edited by S. Dean McBride. Hermeneia. Philadelphia: Fortress Press, 1977.

_____. "The Irresistible Word." *Currents in Theology and Mission* 10 (1983): 4-13.

Wright, T. J. "Amos and the Sycamore Fig." *Vetus Testamentum* 26 (1976): 362-68.

Würthwein, Ernst. "Amos-Studien." *Zeitschrift für die alttestamentliche Wissenschaft* 62 (1950): 10-52.

_____. *The Text of the Old Testament*. Translated by Peter R. Ackroyd. Oxford: Basil Blackwell, 1957.

Yadin, Yigael. "Beer-Sheba. The High Place Destroyed by King Josiah." *Bulletin of the American Schools of Oriental Research* no. 222 (1976): 5-15.

_____. "New Light on Solomon's Megiddo." *The Biblical Archaeologist* 23 (1960): 62-68.

Yadin, Yigael, Yohanan Aharoni, Ruth Amiran, Trude Dothan, Immanuel Dunayevsky, and Jean Perrot. *Hazor 2. An Account of the Second Season of Excavations, 1956.* Jerusalem: Magnes Press, 1960.

Yeivin, S. "The Age of Monarchies." In *Political History,* volume 4 of *World History of the Jewish People,* edited by Abraham Malamat, 162-68. Jerusalem: Masada, 1977.

Zalcman, Lawrence. "Astronomical Illusions in Amos." *Journal of Biblical Literature* 100 (1981): 53-58.

_____. "Piercing the Darkness at *boqer." Vetus Testamentum* 30 (1980): 252-55.

Zeitlin, Solomon. "A Historical Study of the Canonization of the Hebrew Scriptures." In *The Canon and Masorah of the Hebrew Bible,* edited by Sid Z. Leiman, 164-201. New York: KTAV Publishing House, 1974.

Zevit, Ziony. "A Misunderstanding at Bethel, Amos 7:12-17." *Vetus Testamentum* 25 (1975): 783-90.

_____. "Expressing Denial in Biblical Hebrew and Mishnaic Hebrew and in Amos." *Vetus Testamentum* 29 (1979): 505-509.

Ziv, Jehuda. "*Bôqēr Ubôlēs Šikmîm—b'Teqoa?*" [Hebrew]. *Beth Miqra* 28 (1982-1983): 49-53.

Indexes

Subject Index

Scripture Index

Author Index

(*See also* the bibliography, above.)